MFA

HLIGHTS **TEXTILE** & fashion arts

MFA
HIGHLIGHTS **TEXTILE** & fashion arts

PAMELA A. PARMAL

LAUREN D. WHITLEY

SUSAN WARD

ALEXANDRA B. HUFF

TIFFANY WEBBER-HANCHETT

pages 2–3 Detail from a long cover
(see p. 82). *pages 5 and 6* Details
from a *karaori* (see p. 119)

MFA PUBLICATIONS *a division of*
the Museum of Fine Arts, Boston
465 Huntington Avenue
Boston, Massachusetts 02115
tel. 617 369 3438 fax 617 369 3459
www.mfa-publications.org

For a complete listing of MFA
Publications, please contact the
publisher at the above address, or call
617 369 3438.

All photographs are by the Photographic
Studios of the Museum of Fine Arts, Boston,
unless noted otherwise.

Edited by Sarah McGaughey Tremblay
Copyedited by Denise Bergman
Typesetting by Fran Presti-Fazio
Designed and produced by Terry McAweeney
Series design by Lucinda Hitchcock
Printed and bound at CS Graphics PTE LTD,
Singapore

Trade distribution:
Distributed Art Publishers / D.A.P.
155 Sixth Avenue, 2nd floor
New York, New York 10013
Tel. 212 627 1999 Fax 212 627 9484

First edition
Printed in Singapore
This book was printed on acid-free paper

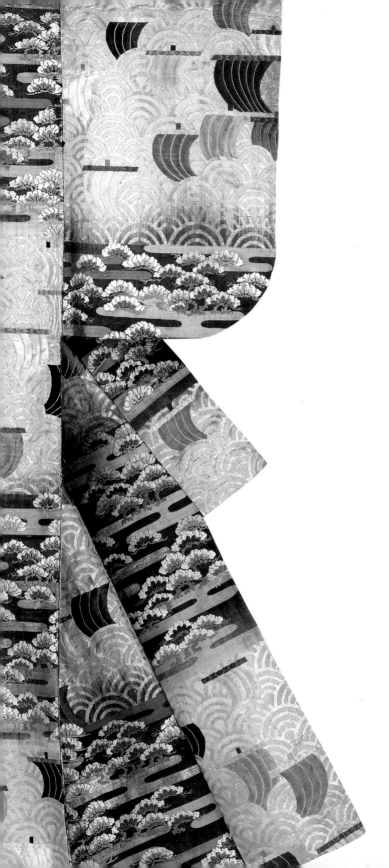

Contents

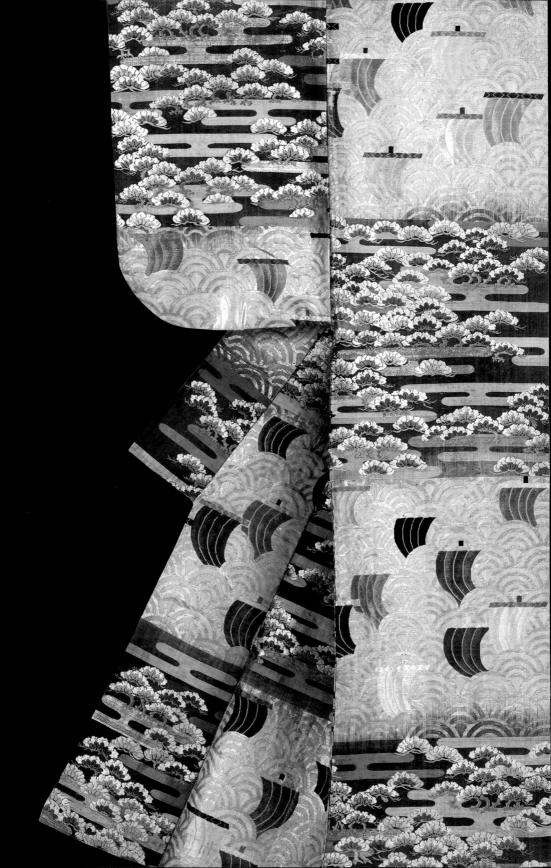

Director's Foreword

Art is for everyone, and it is in this spirit that the MFA Highlights series was conceived. The series introduces some of the greatest works of art in a manner that is both approachable and stimulating. Each volume focuses on an individual collection, allowing fascinating themes—both visual and textual—to emerge. We aim, over time, to represent every one of the Museum's major collections in the Highlights series, thus forming a library that will be a wonderful resource for the understanding and enjoyment of world art.

It is our goal to make the Museum's artworks accessible by every means possible. We hope that each volume of MFA Highlights will help you to know and understand our encyclopedic collections and to make your own discoveries among their riches.

Malcolm Rogers
Ann and Graham Gund Director
Museum of Fine Arts, Boston

Acknowledgments

Choosing one hundred highlights from a collection as broad and deep as that of the Museum of Fine Arts' Textile and Fashion Arts department proved a challenging task, and this book could easily have included twice as many objects. The richness of our holdings is due to the generosity of hundreds of donors, and the department is greatly indebted to them all. Several benefactors require specific acknowledgment in the context of this book. Denman Waldo Ross donated more than four thousand textiles to the MFA between 1876 and 1931, including both the core of our study collection and some of its greatest masterworks. Beginning in 1943, Elizabeth Day McCormick gave more than five thousand textiles, costumes, and costume books and prints. Her donation made the Museum's collection of needlework one of the most important in the world and laid the foundation for the costume collection. Esther Oldham's gift in 1976 of more than four hundred fans from her world-renowned collection brought the Museum similar celebrity. Since the 1960s, John Goelet's generosity and discriminating eye have greatly enriched our holdings of Indian and Persian textiles. More recently, Hannelore and Jeremy Grantham's munificence has allowed us to expand our collections of the magnificent textiles of sub-Saharan Africa and Southeast Asia.

The cultures and traditions discussed in this book are wide-ranging, and we could not have undertaken such a varied study without the expertise and assistance of many colleagues. At the MFA, we would like to thank Lawrence M. Berman, Norma Jean Calderwood Senior Curator of Ancient Egyptian, Nubian, and Near Eastern Art; Anne Havinga, Curator of Photography; Joanna Karlgaard, Research Assistant, Department of Prints, Drawings, and Photographs; Christine Kondoleon, George D. and Margo Behrakis Senior Curator of Greek and Roman Art; Patrick Murphy, Morse Study Room Supervisor; Meghan Melvin, Curatorial Project Assistant, Department of Art of Europe; and Dorie Reents-Budet, Consulting Curator of Pre-Colombian Art. We also extend our gratitude to those outside the Museum who provided advice, including Marianne Aav, Director, Designmuseo, Helsinki; Julia Bailey, Managing Editor, *Muqarnas*, Harvard University; Anna Gonosova, Associate Professor of Art History, UC Irvine; Donna Gorman, Donna Gorman Designs and Marimekko, New Canaan, Connecticut; Ann Rowe, Curator of Western Hemisphere Collection, Textile Museum, Washington, DC; and Jeff Spurr, Islamic and Middle East Specialist, Aga Khan Program, Harvard University.

Many other staff members at the MFA assisted with the project. The Textile Conservation and Collections Care staff—Meredith Montague, Head of Textile Conservation; Claudia Iannuccilli, Associate Conservator; Joel Thompson, Assistant Conservator; and Collections Care Specialists Allison Hewey and Maryann Sadagopan—did a marvelous job preparing the objects for photography. The Museum's photographers, Damon Beale, Greg Heins, David Mathews, and John Woolf, skillfully created the beautiful illustrations of the objects. Sarah McGaughey Tremblay ably and courteously edited the work of five authors, Mark Polizzotti oversaw the publication, Terry McAweeney designed and produced the book, and Christine Pollock coordinated the photography. Hillary Kidd, the Department Assistant in the David and Roberta Logie Department of Textile and Fashion Arts, supported us in the final stages of the project. We thank all of these contributors for their time and talents.

Finally, this book would not have been possible without the help of the National Endowment for the Arts. We are extremely grateful to the NEA for its continued support of the arts and for giving us the opportunity to make the treasures in the Museum's Textile and Fashion Arts collection more accessible.

Pamela A. Parmal
David and Roberta Logie Curator of Textile and Fashion Arts

This book is dedicated to Roberta Logie. Her extraordinary generosity has ensured the future maintenance, accessibility, and growth of the MFA's textile and fashion arts collection.

Textile and Fashion Arts: Their Place in History and in Museums

Pamela A. Parmal

Textiles, and the furnishings and clothing made from them, historically were highly valued necessities of life. People spent much of their work and leisure hours making and adorning textiles that clothed, provided warmth, and, when worn out, filled other utilitarian needs. Luxurious examples were symbols of wealth and position. Some cultures, such as the Han Chinese and the Inca of Peru, attached such importance to textiles that they paid taxes in cloth, while the Kuba of central Africa traded raffia fiber and cloth in lieu of coin. A study of seventeenth- and eighteenth-century probate inventories from colonial New England reveals that textiles, particularly bed furnishings, were among the most precious possessions of the household; colonists regarded their wool hangings, Persian and Turkish carpets, and embroidered linens more highly than the beds, tables, and chairs that they covered.

fig. 1 During the late fifteenth and sixteenth centuries, Europeans prized lavishly patterned velvets embellished with gold metallic thread.

It is difficult for the modern viewer to appreciate the status textiles held prior to the industrialization that occurred during the eighteenth and nineteenth centuries. Today, machines spit out man-made fibers by the mile, and power looms weave yards of complexly patterned cloth in minutes. Before mechanized spinning, jacquard attachments, and computers, every stage in the creation of cloth was accomplished by hand—the harvesting and processing of the fiber, the spinning of the thread, the weaving of the cloth, and, finally, its ornamentation through surface treatments such as printing, embroidery, or resist dyeing. Every step along the way necessitated skill, time, and expensive materials.

In the New England colonies, for example, those who could not afford imported cloth from England needed to produce it themselves. Flax was more easily grown in the Northeast than cotton, and New Englanders commonly used it to produce household linens and clothing. The colonists planted the flax in the spring and harvested it in the fall. They then processed the flax plant through a series of stages to remove the linen fibers contained within the stems. Those

fig. 2 In this fragment of a tapestry from a fifteenth-century set honoring virtuous women, Penelope works at her loom as she awaits the return of her husband, Ulysses.

fig. 3 The basic tools Peruvians used to spin yarns and weave cloth included spindles, picks, shed sticks, whorls, and needles.

steps included drying, rippling (removing the seeds), retting (soaking the plants in water to soften and loosen the woody outer coating), breaking the outer coating, scotching (scraping away the outer coating to reveal the fibers), and finally hackling (combing the fibers). Once the fibers were harvested, they were spun into thread. Women usually did the spinning on small foot-powered wheels called flaxwheels.

After enough thread had been spun to complete a project, the loom was set up. This involved preparing the warp yarns and threading them onto the loom. Women or men often dressed a loom with a warp long enough to enable the completion of numerous projects, such as sheets, towels, table linens, and petticoats or chemises. Finally the weaving could begin. It might proceed relatively quickly if the weaver wove a plain weave, in which the weft was inserted in a simple over and under repeat, but it would move more slowly if the weaver wove a pattern into the cloth. When the weaver finished, the cloth could be further embellished by printing, resist dyeing, or embroidering. Then, at last, it was stitched into a garment or furnishing.

Although much cloth was made at home, those who could afford to buy textiles did so, and a complex industry and trade developed worldwide. Craftsmen specialized in all aspects of cloth and clothing production, including cultivating or importing the fibers, dyeing, weaving, finishing, and embroidering. Meanwhile, merchants, upholsterers, tailors, and dressmakers sold and processed textiles into clothing and furnishings. Specialization occurred where raw materials were located or easily traded. The native Peruvians, for instance, developed sophisticated techniques of working with wool harvested from camelids, such as the llamas and alpacas indigenous to the Andes. They wove, braided, and embroidered brilliantly dyed wool yarns into intricately patterned mantles, tunics, belts, and headdresses. In India, the warm, moist climate suited the growing and processing of long, fine staple cotton, and the country became famous for its intricately dyed-and-fast cotton textiles that were imported into Egypt by the fifth century. Their popularity in Europe during the seventeenth and eighteenth centuries, after oceangoing trade routes had been discovered, completely disrupted the European silk-weaving industries.

Each geographic region and every culture has its own unique textile and clothing history, and we hope that this book will illuminate some of these rich traditions. Its themes include the significance of the textile and apparel industries within the global economy, the value of fine textiles and clothing as status symbols, and the importance of trade in the dissemination of textile patterns and techniques around the world. The book is organized chronologically into four sections. Each contains a series of essays that explore different cultural traditions during that period, including the tapestry fragments of the late Roman world that ornamented clothing and household furnishings, the fabulous carpets of the Islamic world, the dragon robes worn by the Chinese court, and the fashionable garments of postwar couture.

The collection of the Museum of Fine Arts, Boston, provides a wealth of material from which to illustrate a book of this kind. Although classified as a fine arts museum, the MFA has rich holdings of decorative arts that originally developed as study resources for artists and designers. The Museum accessioned textiles of all types, condition, and quality to provide inspiration to students, artists, and designers. These range from a collection of over one hundred decoratively embroidered Yugoslavian sleeve bands to textile masterworks of pre-Columbian Peru. Each essay in this book is illustrated by three or four pieces from the Museum that represent some of the most important and beautiful examples of their kind.

Art, Industry, Education, and Museum Textile Collections
The inclusion of textile collections within the MFA and other major museums in the United States and Europe is a result of the economic importance of the textile industry during the nineteenth century, when most of these museums were founded. In fact, textiles and the development of mechanized textile processes were at the forefront of the eighteenth and nineteenth centuries' Industrial Revolution. During the eighteenth century, manufacturers worked hard to develop mechanized spinning processes, and by 1767 the spinning jenny was

invented, accommodating multiple spindles that could be spun at the same time; the Arkwright water-powered spinning frame followed two years later. By the early nineteenth century, steam-powered looms, roller printing, knitting frames, lace machines, and most importantly, the jacquard attachment, which mechanized the weaving of complex patterns, all revolutionized the industry. Yarn and cloth could now be made in great quantities and at lower prices, making them more widely available and accessible. At the same time, however, many manufacturers paid less attention to good design and quality materials. Textiles, once treasured possessions, became increasingly common and unremarkable.

fig. 4 A combination of old and new printing techniques, including block and engraved roller printing, was used to create this textile commemorating the Great Exhibition of 1851.

Although textile design and craftsmanship went into decline at the majority of the factories producing cloth, not everyone ignored the concepts of good design. Efforts to bring art into industry coincided with the beginning of Western industrialization in the eighteenth century. This was especially true in France, where good design had always been encouraged and supported, within the textile trade in particular. In 1762 the French founded the Ecole des Arts Décoratifs, where students could be taught the principles of good design and art. In England, the Society for the Encouragement of the Arts, Manufactures and Commerce was founded in 1754, but it was not until 1835 that the British government, faced with strong economic competition from other European nations, began to seriously consider the improvement of the country's industrial design. Although the British parliament studied the schools and museums of the Continent, significant progress was not made until after the Great Exhibition of 1851. This exhibition of industrial manufactures, held in the specially constructed glass and steel Crystal Palace in London, was extraordinarily popular and introduced the English to both their own industrial products and those of the rest of the world.

When the doors of the Crystal Palace finally closed, the British were left with great pride in their manufactures and a strong desire to continue to improve their products in order to dominate foreign trade. Acknowledging the need for properly trained artists and designers, and for a museum where the great works of the past might be seen and studied, Parliament finally authorized the formation of the South Kensington School and Museum in 1853. (In 1899 it was renamed the Victoria and Albert Museum.) The aim of South Kensington was to raise design standards in Britain through art education for the purpose of advancing national commerce. It was to be a museum of design, unlike London's National Gallery and Paris's Louvre, both of which primarily collected paintings. South Kensington's industrial design collections would include metalwork, enamels, furniture, pottery and porcelain, glass, textiles, and lace, with an emphasis on acquiring the best works from the past rather than modern pieces.

fig. 5 The MFA's Textile Study Room, established in 1898, provided a place where designers and artists could study the collection.

Art for the sake of education and commerce was something that Americans, who were just beginning to establish museums on their own soil, could appreciate, and the South Kensington School and Museum became a model for the newly founded museums in New York, Philadelphia, Chicago, Providence, Cincinnati, and Boston. When the Museum of Fine Arts, Boston, was incorporated in 1870, one of the primary movers behind its founding, the art theorist and educator Charles Perkins, stated that the Museum's focus should be on "collecting material for the education of a nation in art, not [on] making collections of objects of art." In keeping with this goal, the MFA also incorporated a school and study rooms for designers and artists, including a study room and gallery for textiles.

Denman W. Ross, who taught design at Harvard University and was one of the MFA's textile collection's greatest benefactors, advocated breaking down the established hierarchies between the fine and decorative arts, asking which was more valuable, the work of a first-rate ceramicist or that of a second-rate painter. He believed that in order for artists to understand what was good, they needed to see it, and he strongly encouraged artists and designers to look at art in museums. In 1896 Ross donated almost seven hundred textile fragments from Europe, Persia, and Egypt to the Museum. He wrote in a 1913 article for the Museum *Bulletin*: "The beauty and the value of the object are discovered by comparing it with other objects of the same kind. It is the eye, of course, that tells us what is better and what is best. To know the best of its kind we must have seen it." Over time, Ross's gifts to the textile department totaled more than four thousand pieces and ranged from extraordinary pre-Colombian and colonial Peruvian work to Safavid velvets, European silks, and Egyptian tapestries from the Coptic period. The quality of the gifts ranged as well, from masterworks to derivative copies, in keeping with his philosophy of learning by comparison.

fig. 6 Denman W. Ross's gift of twelve colonial-period pieces, including this tapestry, helped make the Museum's collection of Peruvian textiles one of the most important in the world (detail, see pp. 66–67).

The curators at the MFA, as at the South Kensington Museum, stressed the acquisition of handmade textiles and avoided machine-made work. In 1933 Gertrude Townsend, who had been appointed the MFA's first curator of textiles in 1930, turned down a contemporary printed silk depicting Independence Hall, saying: "The aim of the Textile Department as I understand it, is to collect, preserve and make available for study and enjoyment either in the galleries or in the study room, the best examples of textiles as a fine art, tracing as far as possible, their history and development up to the introduction of modern machine methods." While this strategy clearly suited the designers for whom the Textile Study Room was intended, others who made more frequent use of the facility also benefited, among them art students, embroiderers, weavers, designers for the stage, historians, collectors, and those involved in the growing architecture preservation movement. Townsend understood the important role textiles played historically, economically, and culturally, and she saw beyond the practical use of the collection. She collected not only to provide inspiration to these designers and artists but to document the history of textiles. In doing so, she acquired some of the most important pieces then on the market, including fine Persian silks, medieval tapestries, and ecclesiastical vestments.

fig. 7 When the MFA purchased this masterpiece in 1954, it was the first German tapestry to enter the collection (detail, see pp. 54–55).

fig. 8 Gertrude Townsend led a tour of the Elizabeth Day McCormick collection for representatives of the New York fashion industry in 1944.

Inaugurating Fashion Collections

Most museums in Europe and the United States did not actively collect costume until after World War II, although many pieces entered museums as examples of the textile arts. Morris De Camp Crawford, a writer and early advocate of the use of museum collections by designers, was a leading proponent of the development of a unique American style in both apparel and textiles, one that would be independent of trends in Paris—the acknowledged fashion capital since the seventeenth century. Crawford wrote numerous articles for Women's Wear Daily and was an instigator of the 1916–22 "Designed in America" campaign, which encouraged textile manufacturers and designers to use museum collections for inspiration.

During World War I, the production and dissemination of fashion was briefly interrupted. After the war, to the dismay of Crawford and others who supported American design, ready-to-wear fashion manufacturers and buyers resumed their regular visits to Paris, and that city continued to be the main influence on the American apparel industry. However, World War II and the German occupation of Paris again cut off the flow of French fashion. The work of Crawford and others prior to the war had paved the way for an emerging American style, and American designers such as Claire McCardell, Elizabeth Hawes, Gilbert Adrian, and Irene had already made names for themselves. As the American industry strengthened, a movement grew to develop historical collections to provide inspiration.

Although the Brooklyn Museum collected costume in its early years and opened a study room in 1920, there were no study collections in Manhattan until the 1930s. In 1937 Irene Lewisohn and Alice Lewisohn Crowley founded the Costume Institute, Inc. Both sisters were interested in the theater and felt that a historic collection of costume was a needed resource for the community's designers. The Costume Institute merged with the Metropolitan Museum of Art in 1946 and was heralded as an important resource for the country's apparel designers, as well. It was fully absorbed into the Metropolitan in 1959. The Shirley Goodman Resource Center at the Fashion Institute of Technology was created during the 1960s, and a portion of the Brooklyn Museum's textile and costume study collection was transferred to it. Its location in the center of New York's Seventh Avenue apparel district spoke to its role as a resource for designers.

While New York City was a logical place for fashion collections, Gertrude Townsend established Boston as a destination point when she acquired the McCormick collection of embroidery and costume in 1943. Elizabeth Day McCormick, a member of the Chicago McCormick family, learned to embroider at an early age. She became fascinated by the art and put together a collection of embroidery from around the world. She also became interested in costume, and over the years she collected more than two thousand examples of historical and regional dress, accessories, and fashion plates from the sixteenth to the early nineteenth century. Most of this material came to the MFA in 1943, with additional offerings presented through 1953. McCormick's gifts immediately made the costume collection one of the most important in the country.

Townsend capitalized on her new acquisitions by inviting designers, retailers, and journalists to visit the collection in 1944 and take inspiration from it. The guest book recorded some of the most influential names in New York fashion: Adele Simpson, Nettie Rosenstein, Lily Dache, Polaire Weisman, and Diana Vreeland, among others. Morris De Camp Crawford wrote of the acquisition of the McCormick collection in his 1948 book *The Ways of Fashion*: "If the textile and apparel industries of New England ever reach a recognition of the value of this material and use it properly, there should be a renaissance of the fashion

figs. 9 & 10 **With theatrical backdrops and lighting, the MFA's 1963 exhibition "She Walks in Splendor" was one of the first to examine costume as art, setting the tone for costume exhibitions for the rest of the century.**

arts in New England directly associated with this generous gift." The addition of the collection to the MFA's holdings marked an important shift in the Textile Department's collecting focus and put it more in line with other American museums, which had begun to emphasize the apparel arts.

Adolph Cavallo, who succeeded Townsend as curator of the collection in 1960, saw the costume collection in another light. According to Cavallo, costumes were not just teaching tools or objects for inspiring artists and designers but works of art in their own right. In the catalogue to his seminal 1963 costume exhibition "She Walks in Splendor: Great Costumes, 1550–1950," he declared: "Clothes merely cover and protect the body; but when the wearer chooses or makes those clothes to express a specific idea, then the clothes become *costume* and the whole process, from designing to wearing, becomes art."

By the 1960s, museums like the MFA had begun to reassess the role of costume within their collections. Cavallo's show was one of the earliest and most important fashion exhibitions to celebrate costume as art. The collection was shown against backdrops and lighting created by Broadway designers Raymond Sovey and Horace Armistead. Perry Rathbone, the Museum's director at the time, heralded it as "the most remarkable exhibition of the year, indeed one of the most remarkable in the history of the Museum," as well as perhaps "...the most beautiful and distinguished exhibition of costume ever held anywhere." "She Walks in Splendor" set the tone, in its theatricality and popular appeal, for subsequent exhibitions held at the Costume Institute, many of which were curated by the fashion legend Diana Vreeland, and at the galleries of the Fashion Institute of Technology. These exhibitions enjoyed great popular success from the 1970s through the 1990s.

Cavallo's collecting habits varied from those of his predecessor as he began to actively seek out examples of contemporary fashion and textiles. In 1961 William Filene's Sons Company donated eight ensembles from the couture salon the French Shops. Included in the gift were designs by Nettie Rosenstein, Irene, Princess Irene Galitzine, Antonio Castillo, Cristóbal Balenciaga, James Galanos, and Norman Norell. Cavallo was part of a growing trend. The Victoria and Albert Museum in 1971 invited Cecil Beaton to put together a collection of twentieth-century dress to fill the recognized gap in its collection. Beaton used his many contacts in the theater and fashion world to acquire more than five hundred examples of dress and accessories. In New York, the Metropolitan Museum, the Brooklyn Museum, and the Edward C. Blum Design Laboratory at the Fashion Institute of Technology had already begun to acquire significant examples of twentieth-century fashion and textiles.

Collecting Textiles and Fashion Today

At the beginning of the twenty-first century, academics and scholars in many disciplines have acknowledged the importance of textiles and apparel in the history of trade and economics, while the study of fashion as a cultural and social phenomenon has become a fashion in its own right. Books on fashion theory abound, and exhibitions dealing with issues of gender, ethnicity, and class have been organized in museums around the world.

Textiles and costume collections are no longer seen primarily as a tool to instruct students, designers, and artists but as works of art and important cultural and historical documents. Gertrude Townsend understood this, and although the MFA originally employed her to oversee the development of the collection to meet the needs of artists and industrial designers, Townsend's writings and her collecting strategy show that she was at the forefront of the study of textile history and she formed the collection accordingly. Her successors have made significant attempts to bring the holdings into the future and have acknowledged the importance of textiles and dress in the industrial and postindustrial periods, as can be seen in the final section of this book. The collection will continue to grow and its uses to evolve, but as in the past, curators will focus their attention on collecting the finest examples of the textile and fashion arts in order to inspire, instruct, and astound.

Antique and Medieval Textiles 700 B.C.–A.D. 1500

As soon as men and women first began to hunt and gather, they developed spinning, weaving, and other textile techniques, making the most of the materials available to them locally. They wove reeds and grasses into mats and baskets; knotted, plaited, and wove linen and bast fibers into cords, bags, and bands; and tailored animal skins into practical garments. Inhabitants of sub-Saharan Africa made beaten bark-cloth loincloths and plaited raffia skirts for protection and for ceremonies. In South America, the people of the Andes spun and wove the wool of llamas and alpacas to make clothing suitable for their cooler climate. Cultures around the world developed other indigenous fibers including linen, which people in Turkey, Iran, Iraq, and Egypt began preparing before the fifth millennium B.C., and silk, which the Chinese have cultivated since at least the third millennium B.C.

As people became more sedentary and economies advanced, textile technologies multiplied and lavishly woven and decorated cloths became symbols of wealth and power. Merchants established complex trade routes by the fifth century B.C., bringing silks from China along the Silk Road as far west as Greece and cottons from India to Egypt and the Mediterranean. These exotic imports were highly sought after and in turn inspired new technologies where they were imported. The early history of textiles is complex and still not completely understood, but the fabrics that have survived the vicissitudes of nature point to an extremely rich and varied past.

fig. 11 This ancient Greek woman straightens wool fibers into a loose bundle called a roving, a preliminary step before spinning fibers into yarns.

Paracas Textiles

Between 300 B.C. and A.D. 300, a culture now called Paracas flourished in southern Peru. We know of these people who inhabited the fertile lower Ica Valley and the desert coast of Peru through the archaeological record of their ceramics and textiles. Surviving Paracas textiles provide a small but extremely impressive record of their makers' accomplishments; in fact, the textiles exhibit almost every nonmachine textile technique known.

Archaeologists became aware of the Paracas culture in the first decades of the twentieth century, when ceramics and elaborately embroidered textiles came onto the market and into the collections of antiquaries and museums. In 1925, they discovered the location from which these magnificent textiles originated. It was a dry desert peninsula on the south coast of Peru, known by the Quechua word *para-ako* because of the strong wind of the same name that blew across during the afternoon. The name Paracas became associated with the culture that lived there and, more significantly, used the area as a burial ground. The Paracas people could not have chosen a better spot to ensure the survival of their cultural remains, as the extremely dry climate preserved the mummy bundles they buried in underground rooms.

Most of the surviving Paracas textiles originally wrapped mummy bundles found in high-status burials that reflected the power and position of the wearer. Paracas textile scholar Anne Paul has identified the type of textiles that are in the MFA's collection as ritual attire. Men wore several styles of garments including mantles, which they draped over their shoulders as their outer and most spectacular garment. They also wore loincloths, ponchos, tunics, and head cloths or turbans. Artisans embroidered elaborate high-status garments with anthropomorphic figures that conveyed information about the social, religious, and environmental life of the Paracas people.

Researchers have identified two primary styles of embroidery: the color-block style and the linear style. The color-block style is exemplified by the mantle on page 28 decorated with bird impersonators. When working this type of embroidery, the artist first outlined the figure in wool, then filled in the background, and finally completed the figures with colored wool. According to current scholarship, this type of embroidery was appropriate to textiles that depicted images related to the individual's role in society, such as bird impersonators who may have danced or performed during ritual ceremonies.

The bird impersonators may represent falcons or condors, powerful predators who captured their prey during the day. By impersonating these mighty creatures of the sky, the men may have endowed themselves with their strength as hunters and warriors. They may also have viewed birds that inhabited the sky as metaphors for passage to the celestial realm. Artists derived all of the figures they embroidered onto ritual attire from the natural and mythological world. Other subjects included the lima bean, killer whale, shark, hummingbird, pampas cat, and yam bean.

The poncho illustrated on page 29 exemplifies the linear style, which is characterized by fewer colors, one of them the same as the background. This style

resulted in images that are often difficult to read and could indicate the communication of more abstract ideas, in contrast to the actual depiction of cult figures in color-block embroideries. The maker of this poncho embroidered two-headed birds, with a series of smaller and smaller birds "nesting" inside the larger figures. Unfortunately, the meaning of this image is now lost to us.

Although most of the textiles that have come to us from the Paracas burials were worn as ritual attire, the Paracas people and their neighbors on the south coast widely used other types of cloth. Large hangings made in the extremely complex technique of discontinuous warp and weft weaving are among the more spectacular survivals. Only two such hangings are known, both of which are fragmentary. One is shown on page 30; the other is in the Brooklyn Museum. Our example contains imagery similar to that of ritual attire, such as flying anthropomorphic figures. The figure on the far left wears a striped skirt that often symbolized the tail of the falcon and may indicate that the figure is a mythological being with bird attributes.

PAP

Man's mantle

Paracas culture

Peru (South Coast), A.D. 50–100

Wool plain weave, embroidered with wool

a: 101 x 244.3 cm (39¾ x 96¼ in.)

b: 13.3 x 241.9 cm (5¼ x 95¼ in.)

c: 14 x 25.2 cm (5½ x 10 in.)

Denman Waldo Ross Collection   16.34a–c

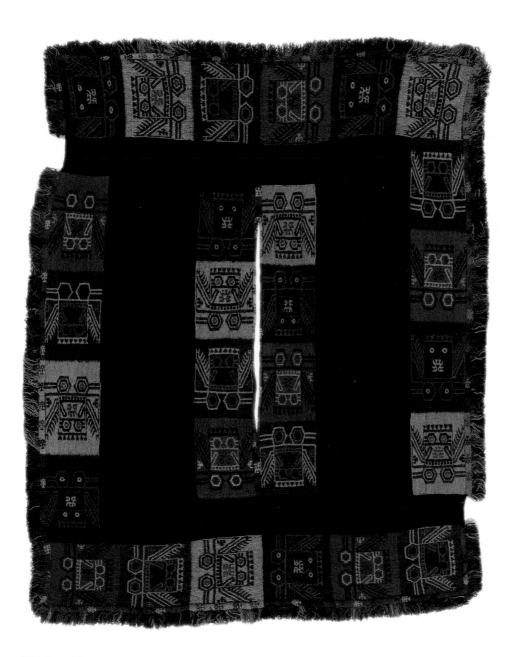

Man's poncho
Paracas culture
Peru (South Coast), 100 B.C.–0
Wool plain weave, embroidered with wool
64.8 x 50.8 cm (25 ½ x 20 in.)
Mary Woodman Fund   31.496

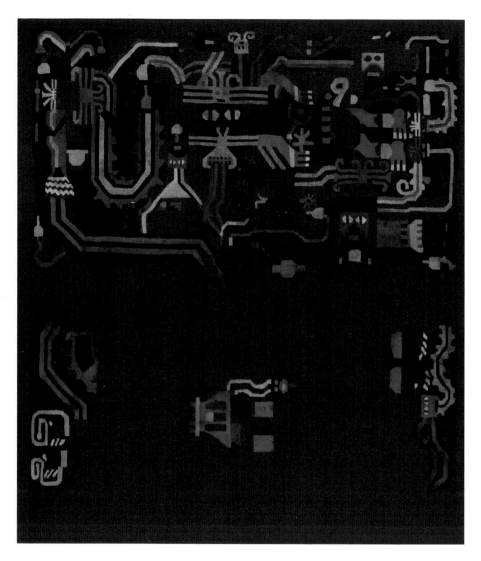

Fragments of a hanging

Peru (South Coast)

Paracas-Nasca transition, about A.D. 200

Wool plain weave with discontinuous warps
and wefts

a: 69.9 x 113.6 cm (27½ x 44¾ in.)

b: 58.5 x 19 cm (23 x 7½ in.)

c: 21.5 x 29 cm (8½ x 11½ in.)

d: 45 x 18.5 cm (17½ x 7¼ in.)

Edwin E. Jack Fund   67.313a–d

Late Antique Textiles

In Roman antiquity, ornately decorated textiles enriched domestic and other interiors as curtains, hangings, carpets, covers, and pillows, as well as ornamenting clothing. The fabrics were most commonly made of wool and linen, although weavers also used silk and cotton yarns imported from central Asia, China, and India. The textiles shared decorative motifs and figural themes, which could be woven, embroidered, dyed, or painted, with other categories of Roman art. It is assumed that these fabrics were made all over the Roman Empire, although the vast majority of surviving textiles were found in the burial grounds of late Roman and early medieval Egypt. The MFA's collection consists of a rich sampling of these textiles, from nearly complete pieces to small fragments.

This tapestry-woven neck ornament with a jeweled neck band and end panels decorated with mythological figures on a purple ground illustrates the richness of clothing decoration. Originally part of a linen tunic, the ornament is woven in fine wool, linen, and gold-wrapped silk yarns. The tapestry weaver enhanced the richness of the design by using gold-wrapped thread as well as vividly dyed wool yarns. The purple wool of the ground could be Tyrian purple, the finest and most expensive dye of antiquity, which was extracted from a species of eastern Mediterranean mollusk and was originally made famous by the Phoenicians of Tyre, in present-day Lebanon. The figural motifs are woven in an illusionistic style widespread in figural representations of the third and fourth centuries.

Two large textiles, a linen cover decorated with roundels and bands (p. 34) and a curtain fragment depicting a seated Dionysus (p. 35), exemplify the decorative range of Late Antique textiles. The almost intact rectangular linen cloth carries five large roundels and two pairs of border bands woven in tapestry weave in purple-brown wool. The wool was dyed not with Tyrian purple but rather with cheaper dyes such as madder top-dyed with indigo. Complex geometric and interlace patterns were extremely common on textiles with this purple background, though artists sometimes used figural designs instead. Here, geometric and interlace designs crafted in linen and woolen threads fill the roundels and bands. The pattern decorating the central roundels may have been more than a decoration, perhaps acting as a defense against the evil eye by trapping the gaze within its intricate design.

The large fragment portraying Dionysus shows the pagan god of wine seated beneath an arch, probably a niche, with a panther at his feet. It was likely the central portion of a large linen curtain that included Dionysus's companions under similar arches. Two segments of that curtain are preserved—one, in the Cleveland Museum of Art, shows a satyr with a maenad, and the other, in the Abbegg Foundation in Riggisberg, Switzerland, illustrates a kithara player. The curtain's maker wove Dionysus and his companions in wool tapestry in a colorful, illusionistic style similar to contemporary monumental paintings and floor mosaics. Curtains such as this were common in late antiquity and may have been used as an alternative to wall paintings or as closures for the porticoes popular in domestic architecture. Many were decorated with mythological subjects, and the myth of Dionysus was particularly popular. Artists frequently included Dionysiac themes in all kinds of textiles and in Roman and Late Antique art in general, perhaps because they had an auspicious meaning.

A small fragment depicting a seated shepherd amid his flock (p. 35) is an example of rarer silk fabrics. Between the fourth and sixth centuries, merchants imported silk from Asia (either Sasanian Iran or China) as yarns and as woven fabrics. This small piece represents the silk textiles that may have been woven in Egypt or the eastern Mediterranean, which shared motifs and themes with textiles made from other fibers. Pastoral themes occurred often in Roman and Late Antique art. The repeated motifs could be ornamental or figural as in this piece. Frequently they were woven in two or three colors only. This silk fragment is too small to determine its original use. It might have been used as an applied decoration on an article of clothing such as a tunic, or it may be a fragment of a larger textile.

PAP

Neck ornament

Found in Egypt
Late Antique period, 4th century
Wool, linen, and gold-wrapped
silk thread slit tapestry
56.9 x 15.8 cm (22⅜ x 6¼ in.)
Charles Potter Kling Fund 46.401

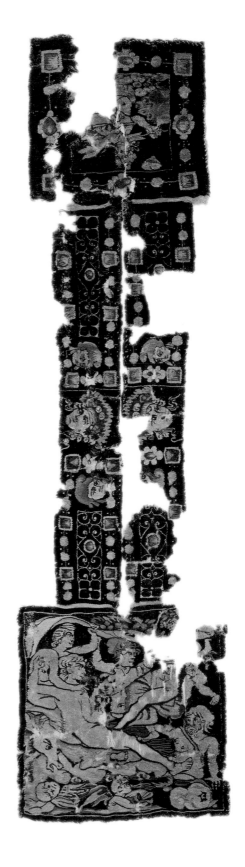

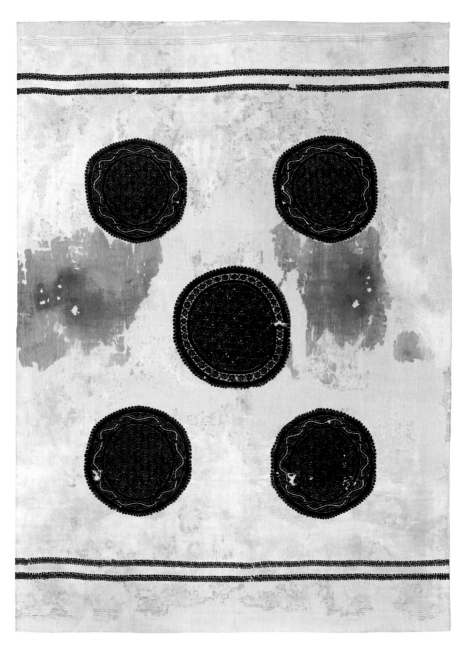

Cover

Egypt (found at Akmin)

Late Antique period, 4th–5th century

Linen plain weave with wool

tapestry insertions

312.4 cm x 222.3 cm (123 x 87½ in.)

Denman Waldo Ross Collection   94.120

Dionysus fragment from a hanging

Possibly from Egypt

Late Antique period, 4th–5th century

Linen plain weave with wool

tapestry insertions

139 x 79 cm (54¾ x 31⅛ in.)

Charles Potter Kling Fund   1973.290

Silk fragment

Probably found in Egypt

Late Antique period, 4th century

Silk compound weft twill (samite)

7.2 x 9 cm (2¹³/₁₆ x 3⁹/₁₆ in.)

Denman Waldo Ross Collection   11.90

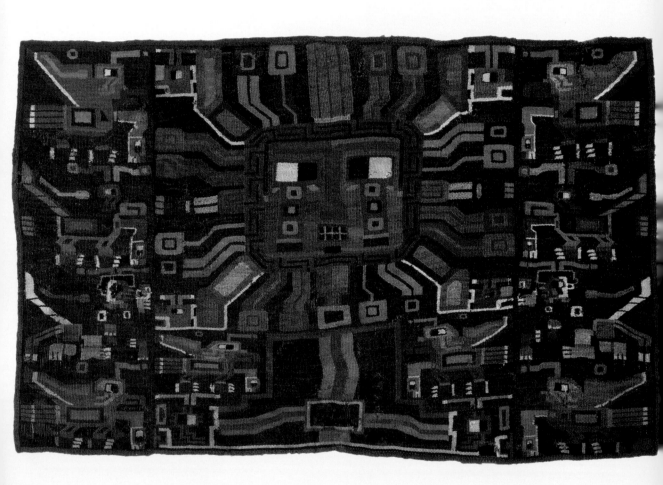

Tapestry panel from a Tiwanaku-style tunic
Possibly Pukara culture
Peru, A.D. 250–450
Wool (camelid) tapestry
48.9 x 77.5 cm (19¼ x 30½ in.)
Charles Potter Kling Fund   1994.203

Tiwanaku-Style and Wari Textiles

In the highlands of Bolivia, at the southern tip of the deep mountain lake Titicaca, an expansive ceremonial center flourished from A.D. 200 to 1000. One of the most striking architectural features of the site is the Gateway of the Sun. Ancient sculptors carved the image of a deity in the center of the gateway's lintel. Rays terminating in circles and feline heads surround his head, tear tracks are visible under his eyes, and he bears a staff in each hand. Scholars alternately refer to the deity as the God of the Sun, Moon, or Stars. The rayed head also appears on lavishly patterned tunics and mantles made of tapestry-woven camelid fiber. Specialists identify these garments as Tiwanaku-style, after the civilization that prospered in the area between A.D. 750 and 1000. Researchers have carbon-dated several of the tunics and tunic fragments to A.D. 250–450 and have suggested that they were made by the Pukara people, who thrived in the area at the turn of the millennium.

The tapestry-woven panel shown here would have been incorporated into such a tunic at the shoulder. An identical panel would have been inserted on the opposite shoulder. In the center of the panel, a rayed face with tear tracks sits atop a stepped platform that resembles the ceremonial temples built near Lake Titicaca. The appendages encircling the head terminate in puma heads, and bird-headed attendants surround the deity. Several similar pairs of panels survive, as does a tunic with panels incorporated at the shoulders. That tunic has a field of red wool, and its maker attached tapestry bands with trophy heads at the bottom hem and at the armhole. Only the elite would have worn tunics in this style, probably in association with rituals related to their political, spiritual, or economic life.

The Tiwanaku style influenced other South American peoples as far south as Arica, Chile, and as far east as the Peruvian coast. The Wari, who lived throughout Peru from about A.D. 750 to 950, seem to have adopted religious practices and associated imagery and burial customs similar to those of the Tiwanaku people. These practices included making four-cornered hats to top mummy bundles and weaving elaborate tapestry tunics depicting staff-bearing figures for the mummies. The four-cornered hat illustrated on page 38 resembles those of the Tiwanaku in design but differs from them in technique. It is made of knotted cotton covered with brilliantly dyed wool pile that creates a design of composite bird-camelid figures. Tiwanaku hats are characterized by a tightly knotted surface, usually without pile.

The most elaborate Wari mummy bundles contained intricately woven tapestry tunics that depict staff-bearing figures similar to those flanking the main deity on the Tiwanaku Gateway of the Sun. Large tie-dyed mantles like the one on page 39 often accompanied the tunics. These extremely graphic textiles are the result of complicated and time-consuming techniques. Discontinuous warp and weft weaving had developed during the Paracas-Nasca transition period. This textile's maker employed that technique to facilitate tie-dyeing the piece in multiple colors. After weaving the textile, the artist took apart the independent stepped sections, tie-dyed them to create diamond shapes against a different-colored background, and then sewed them together by dovetailing the warps and stitching the weft slits together.

PAP

Four-cornered hat

Wari culture

Peru, Middle Horizon period, A.D. 700–900

Knotted cotton ground with wool (camelid) pile

11.4 x 47.5 cm (4 ½ x 18¹¹⁄₁₆ in.)

Mrs. Cabot's Special Fund   47.1096

Mantle

Wari culture

Peru, Middle Horizon period, A.D. 700–900

Wool (camelid) plain weave with discontinuous
warps and wefts, disassembled, tie-dyed, and
reassembled

114 x 187 cm (44⅞ x 73⅝ in.)

Textile Fund and Helen and Alice Colburn Fund

1983.252

Medieval Islamic Textiles

Textiles have long played an important role within Islamic culture. Rulers presented textiles and clothing as diplomatic gifts and as tokens of favor within the court; members of the court prized the lavishly patterned silks, which served as symbols of authority, wealth, and prestige. In addition, textiles were significant within the domestic sphere; families liberally furnished their homes with beautiful divan covers, pillows, cushions, storage bags, and sacks. When Islam spread throughout the Near and Middle East and the Levant in the seventh century, silk weaving was already well established in Mesopotamia, Iran, and northern Syria. As these centers came under Islamic control, silk production continued and textiles became one of the Islamic world's most important manufactured and traded goods. As Islam expanded north and west—as far as Spain by the early eighth century—sericulture and silk weaving techniques traveled as well. From Persia, they migrated northwest to Armenia and south to Fars, while from northern Syria sericulture traveled south to North Africa and then on to Spain and into Sicily.

Islamic proscriptions against the depiction of living things, seen as an attempt to rival the Creator, did not always apply to the adornment of textiles. In the early Islamic period, figured fabrics were allowed as long as the images were not associated with religious veneration. Repeating roundels that enclosed animal and human figures were one of the most common designs. This type of pattern appeared as early as the sixth century in Iran and Mesopotamia, and its pop-

ularity spread to central Asia, China, Byzantium, North Africa, and Europe. The two beautiful examples illustrated on page 42 are associated with Tabriz and Baghdad.

The small fragment reportedly found near Tabriz, in northwestern Iran, illustrates the refinement of eleventh-century Islamic silk design. It contains a portion of a roundel whose border is decorated with the Islamic inscription "lasting glory, all-embracing bounty, felicity, good fortune, and abundant ease to the owner." The rest of the fragment shows a beautifully drawn falcon's head. A larger piece in the collection of the Berlin Kunstgewerbe Museum shows that a second falcon would have faced the first.

The other fragment embroidered with repeating roundels, reportedly excavated in Baghdad, illustrates why that city was fabled for beautiful cloth. Although the textile is now extremely discolored and incomplete, it still offers a glimpse of its original magnificence. Repeating roundels each enclose a different animal. The most complete one features a peacock; the others surround a lion and a winged horse. When the Museum originally acquired the piece, a second fragment, whose present location is unknown, provided evidence of two borders. One border included a Kufic inscription—unfortunately unreadable. The second border was patterned with tangent circles that also included animals. This design layout indicates that the textile could originally have been used as furnishing fabric and may be a rare survival of the fabled wall hangings referred to in literature such as *The Arabian Nights*.

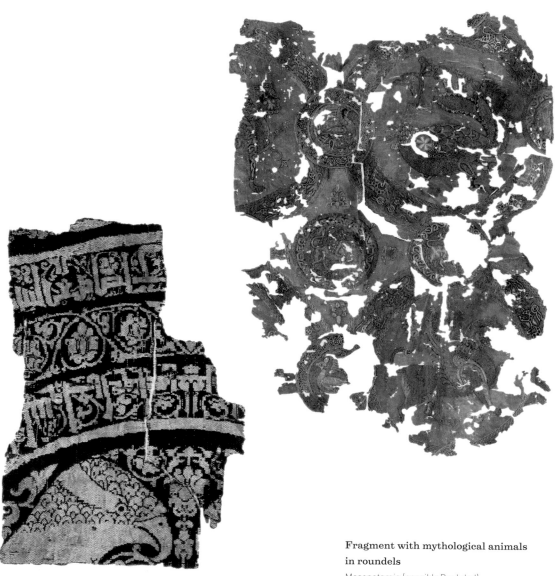

Fragment with paired falcons in roundel

Iran (possibly Tabriz)

11th–12th century

Silk double cloth

20 x 14 cm (7 ⅞ x 5 ½ in.)

Denman Waldo Ross Collection 04.1621

Fragment with mythological animals in roundels

Mesopotamia (possibly Baghdad)

10th–11th century

Silk and cotton plain weave (*mulham*), embroidered with silk and metal-wrapped thread

68.5 x 50.5 cm (27 x 19 in.)

Archibald Cary Coolidge Fund 37.103

Another piece, from Spain, illustrates just how far textiles traveled and their influence extended. This fragment of silk is from the burial shroud of San Pedro de Osma from the cathedral of Burgo de Osma in Spain. It is patterned with rows of tangential roundels enclosing wrestling lions and harpies. Medallions link the roundels, and floral designs fill the diamond shapes. All of these elements also appear in the embroidered fragment from Baghdad. Although its design is Persian, this textile shows characteristics of cloth woven in southern Spain, particularly those made in Almería, where a lucrative industry developed in the twelfth century. Almerían silks are characterized by the colors red, green, and gold, and their makers brocaded isolated elements with metal-wrapped thread, such as the faces of the harpies and the lions on this example.

What makes this piece unique is the Arabic inscription woven into the small medallions, which has been translated as "This was made in Baghdad, may God watch over it." Initially the textile was considered Mesopotamian, but its similarities to other textiles woven in Almería, as well as the typically Hispanic style of the inscription, points to a Spanish origin. Records from twelfth-century Spain document the use of false inscriptions on textiles, pointing to the value of Baghdad silks throughout the Islamic world and acknowledging the popularity of textiles patterned with repeating roundels.

PAP

Fragment with wrestling lions and harpies
Spain (probably Almería)
Early 12th century
Silk lampas with supplementary discontinuous
metal-wrapped patterning wefts
50 x 43 cm (19¾ x 17 in.)
Ellen Page Hall Fund   33.371

Medieval Silks for the Church

Gold and silk threads glistened in the candlelit interiors of churches all over Europe during the Middle Ages, in garments for priests and in coverings for altars and reliquaries. As the most powerful institution in the West, the church was a focal point for people from all walks of life; the church calendar structured the seasons, days, and even hours. People gathered to celebrate the Mass, the most important church ritual, in cathedrals and in humbler chapels where colorful woven and embroidered fabrics adorned the fronts of altars. Like painted decoration, textile panels told stories about biblical figures and popular saints. Fabric bags and reliquary covers protected the physical remains of holy people, as the veneration of relics gained widespread popularity, offering support and comfort to people confronted with the harsh realities of life in that time.

Clothing worn by church officials was among the most lavish in society, later influencing the coronation dress of kings and emperors. The chasuble and miter illustrated in this section, both from the church of Saint Peter in Salzburg, Austria, hint at the grand impression such vestments would have made. Twelfth-century chasubles were cone shaped, constructed from a half circle of fabric brought together and seamed along the front, leaving a hole at the top for the head. Designers often decorated the neck, front seam, back, and shoulders with fabric bands called orphreys that formed a fork-shaped cross on the front and back of the garment. Circles at the cruxes of the orphreys probably once held semiprecious stones.

Chasuble from the abbey church of the Benedictine monastery of Saint Peter
Austria (Salzburg)
11th century, with 12th-century repairs
Silk compound weft twill (samite), embroidered with metal-wrapped thread and applied tablet-woven bands
Center back length: 153 cm (60¼ in.)
Ellen Frances Mason Fund   33.676

Islamic weavers likely made the chasuble's original dark blue silk in what is today southern Turkey. An inscription woven into the fabric itself reads, in Arabic, "Great is Allah." Though it may seem surprising to find an Arabic inscription on a textile used in a Western Christian church, such cultural crossover was not uncommon in the Middle Ages. Christian artisans working in both Byzantium and the West frequently adopted Islamic decorative motifs.

While such an abundance of lushly draped silk must have created a grand impression, practical considerations like freedom of movement led to the gradual modification of chasubles into the more abbreviated, armless style still used today. Many medieval chasubles were reworked into the later style, but the Latin inscription around the bottom of this one probably saved it from that fate. To create it, the maker utilized gold-wrapped threads, tacking them down with surface couching and then hammering them to create an overall glossy surface. The writing can be translated roughly as "Heinrich, the sinner, completed this noble garment for Saint Peter's altar, that it may be his helper." The humble Heinrich may have been the church official who commissioned the chasuble or a wealthy patron who donated it.

Just as the chasuble was the symbolic outer garment of bishops, the miter was the ceremonial headdress that only bishops—and some abbots by special arrangement of the pope—could wear. Abbots at Saint Peter's in Salzburg were granted this privilege in 1231. This miter is an early example of the two-pointed style that evolved in the late twelfth century. The points symbolize the Old and New Testaments, and the two lappets, or ribbons, hung down the wearer's back. Like the chasuble, this miter is decorated with orphreys, as well as couched gold-wrapped thread and silk embroidery.

**Miter from the abbey church of the
Benedictine monastery of Saint Peter**
Austria (Salzburg)
13th century
Silk lampas, embroidered with silk and
metal-wrapped thread; tablet-woven lappets
Miter: 22.5 x 28 cm (8⅞ x 11 in.)
Lappets: 48 x 6 cm (18⅞ x 2⅜ in.)
Helen and Alice Colburn Fund 38.887

A very different kind of embroidery was used to create the pictorial panel illustrated here. Artists created such "pictures in silk" on a plain linen ground throughout Europe in the Middle Ages, most famously in England in a style known as *opus Anglicanum*. This example probably was made in Italy in the fourteenth century, based on comparisons with contemporary painting and manuscript illumination, and was once part of a set that adorned a larger piece, either a clerical garment or an altar hanging.

The scene on the right of the panel may depict the Second Council of Lyons, held in 1274. At that council, the Byzantine emperor, Michael Paleologus VIII, ceded authority to the reigning pope, Gregory X, thus temporarily mending what had been a long-standing schism between the Byzantine and Western churches. The figure with the key—the traditional symbol of Saint Peter, who passed legitimate church rule from pope to pope—may be Saint Bonaventure, who was instrumental in Gregory's papal election. Bonaventure died in 1274, the year of the Lyons council, so if this interpretation is correct it is likely his burial that is depicted at the left of the scene.

Embroidered panel

Probably Italy

14th century

Linen plain weave, embroidered with

silk and metal-wrapped thread

35 x 49.3 cm (13¾ x 19½ in.)

Otis Norcross Fund 46.1198

Other medieval textiles had a functional relationship with death and the deceased as reliquary containers. This finely embroidered panel from a church treasury in Mainz, Germany, once formed the front of a small bag that likely contained a precious relic. The heraldic shields and motifs, in a sampler-like array of various stitches and types of drawn work, are characteristic of German embroidery of the thirteenth century. Although the name on the front of the bag, "Hadevigis," might identify the saint whose remains were kept inside, it may also refer to the object's maker. Another inscription on the reverse of the panel reads: "Hadewigis me fecit," Latin for "Hadewig made me."

As this signed bag and the inscribed chasuble indicate, it is a myth that all medieval art was anonymous. Though the names of most medieval artisans are lost to us, numerous patrons' and artists' names do appear on sculpture, in illuminated manuscripts, and on textiles. These names attest to the timelessness of human pride in artistic accomplishment.

ABH

Fragment of a relic bag
Germany (probably Mainz)
13th century
Linen gauze, embroidered with silk
20 x 18 cm (8 x 7 in.)
Gift of Mrs. Charles Gaston Smith's Group
39.543

European Medieval Tapestries

Tapestries were the most sought-after, expensive, and important luxury items of the later Middle Ages in northern Europe. Royal inventories indicate that they were far more important than paintings. In addition to displaying the owner's wealth and status, tapestries kept out drafts and served as backdrops for religious ceremonies and theatrical productions. Because they were portable, their owners used them as room dividers, brought them on military campaigns and set them up in tents, and hung them on building facades on special feast days.

Technically speaking, a tapestry is a textile patterned with discontinuous wefts. (One of the most famous medieval textiles, known as the "Bayeaux tapestry," in fact is not a tapestry at all but rather an embroidery.) To begin a tapestry, a team of weavers stretched undyed yarns (the warp) on a loom. A full-scale design plan, called a cartoon, was either hung on the wall for reference or placed under the yarns and traced with ink directly onto the warp. The artisans then completely covered the warp with colored yarns (the weft), weaving them over and under the warp yarns in accordance with the colors and patterns specified on the cartoon. If differently colored weft yarns passed around adjacent warps without linking, vertical openings or slits were created, lending the name "slit tapestry" to this kind of weaving. These slits were sometimes a desirable means of adding depth and shadow to the finished piece, though weavers could also sew the slits together or use a technique called

dovetailing to interlock the wefts around a common warp. Tapestry weaving was extremely time-consuming. An expert weaver could complete about one square inch of work in an hour, and it would have taken a group of artisans working full-time many months to create each of the three tapestries shown in this section.

Over the centuries, these three works have acquired titles that describe the scenes they depict. Like all medieval images, however, those in tapestries could have multiple meanings. Pictures functioned symbolically in the Middle Ages, so that a person or thing

depicted might have both a literal meaning and an allegorical significance intended to teach people about some higher religious or moral truth. These three tapestries, fashioned at the artistic height of tapestry production in the fifteenth century, illustrate how such symbolism could be used in varying ways.

The First Four Articles of the Creed depicts symbolic relationships between Old Testament prophesies and the Apostles' Creed, an affirmation of the Catholic faith. According to tradition, each of the twelve sections, or articles, of the Creed was attrib-

The First Four Articles of the Creed

Flanders (probably Brussels)
About 1475–1500
Wool and silk slit tapestry
427 x 833 cm (168 x 328 in.)
Gift of Mrs. John Harvey Wright in memory of her son
Eben Wright and her father Lyman Nichols 08.441

uted to one of the twelve apostles. This tapestry is divided into four bays representing the first four articles, indicating that it was originally part of a set of three. In the first bay, in the lower left, the prophet Jeremiah holds a scroll stating, "We shall call you the Father who made the earth and the heavens." His words are positioned as a symbolic foreshadowing of those attributed to the apostle Peter. Saint Peter sits to the prophet's right wearing glasses (clearly anachronistic for the apostle's time, though eyeglasses had been depicted in the West since the mid-fourteenth century). A scroll above him reads: "I believe in God the Father Almighty, maker of heaven and earth," the opening article of the Creed. The accompanying scene above shows God the Father creating Eve from Adam's side. Similar parallels between the Old and New Testaments are drawn in each of the other bays, illustrated with scenes of the Baptism of Christ, the Nativity, and the Crucifixion.

Unlike the *Creed*, the early fifteenth-century German tapestry *Wild Men and Moors* was probably conceived as a stand-alone work. While the frenetic energy and all-over surface pattern are initially challenging to the viewer, careful observation reveals that the scene is balanced and ordered and makes rich use of symbolism. From left to right, hairy wild men invade a castle, struggle with beasts (including a lion, dragon, and unicorn), and bring gifts of food to a wild woman and her children. The whole composition can be read as the triumph of domesticity over warlike behavior. Furthermore, the castle and the "chain" pattern of the background may allude to contemporary notions of courtly love, in which unattainable ladies kept hapless lovers captive in the bonds of desire. Religious allegory can also be construed: the unicorn was often a symbol of Christ, and the mother-child pair may be a rustic version of the nativity scene.

The theme of taming nature appears again in *Narcissus* (p. 56), a tapestry designed in the popular decorative style known as *millefleurs*. Featuring figures set against a richly patterned botanical background, *millefleurs* works symbolically domesticated the wild by turning it into artifice. At the same time, this piece documents the developing interest in scientific observation: the artist copied the numerous species of plants and creatures depicted in the dense background so carefully from nature that many can be botanically identified. The subject of Narcissus derives from Ovid's *Metamorphoses*. Medieval and Renaissance thinkers rediscovered and reinterpreted

tales by classical authors allegorically as moral lessons for a Christian audience. In the story of Narcissus, the gods trick a handsome young man into falling in love with his own reflection. In our post-Freudian world, we associate narcissism with neurotic self-absorption, but the lesson for medieval viewers focused on the perils of idolatry and the seductive power of images.

ABH

Wild Men and Moors

Germany (probably Strasbourg, Alsace)
About 1440
Linen and wool slit tapestry
100 x 490 cm (39¼ x 193 in.)
Charles Potter Kling Fund 54.1431

Narcissus

France or Flanders

About 1480–1520

Wool and silk slit tapestry

282 x 311 cm (111 x 122 ½ in.)

Charles Potter Kling Fund   68.114

The Age of Exploration 1500–1750

After the Portuguese first landed on the Gold Coast of Africa in 1471, Christopher Columbus happened upon the New World in 1492, and Ferdinand Magellan's ship returned from circumnavigating the globe for the first time in 1522, Europeans quickly established oceangoing trade routes. These routes competed with the profitable overland passages through central Asia and the Middle East, giving the Europeans direct access to the spices and silks of Asia and gold from Africa and South America. These explorations profoundly altered the global economy, in which the textile trade played a central role.

Silks from China and cottons from India did occasionally reach Europe prior to 1500, but they were rare and exotic luxuries. When European ships began to trade with China, Japan, and India, textiles and the fibers and dyes used to make them became important commodities. Soon large quantities of Indian printed and painted cottons were imported into Europe and began to rival European textiles in popularity. The indigenous textiles and other exotic goods that seafarers brought back from Indonesia, Japan, and China inspired a fascination with the exotic East and spurred a fashion for orientalist design in Europe. Contact between Asia and Europe also introduced European designs to the courts of India and Asia, where they in turn inspired local artisans. The textiles from this period demonstrate this globalization. Carpets of the Mughal court, dress silks of France and Holland, and velvets of the Ottoman court are all tangible evidence of exploration and the profound influences of one civilization on another.

fig. 12 Many Europeans traded in China through the port of Canton. In this view of the harbor, the ships fly the flags of the Netherlands, Sweden, and Denmark.

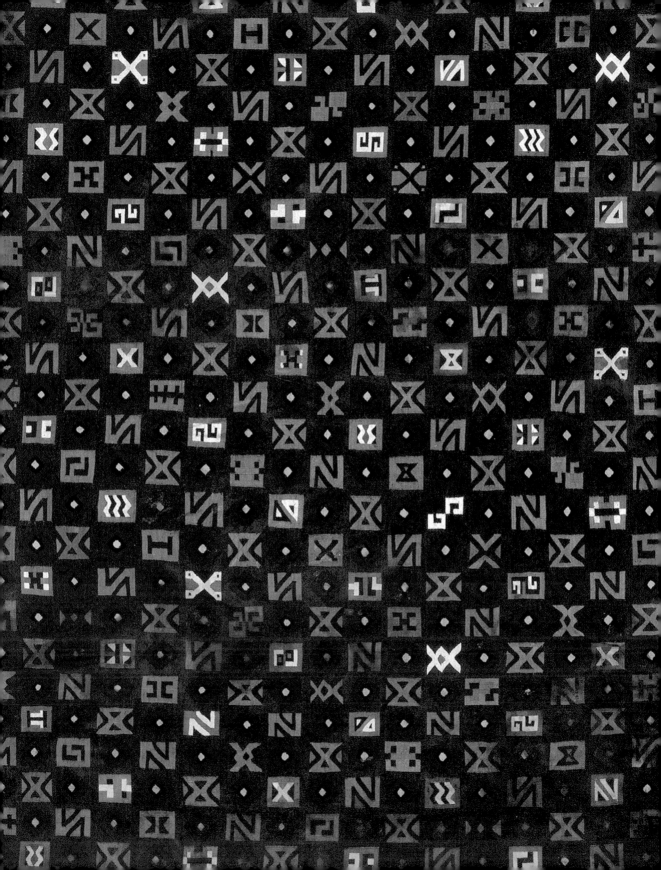

Postconquest Andean Textiles

When Spanish soldiers arrived in the Andes region of western South America in 1532, they encountered a thriving Inca empire whose aesthetic, political, and economic foundations centered on textile production and distribution. The Spanish were quick to appreciate the virtuosity of Inca textiles, and they began a process of domination that would bring the Inca tribute system under their control. Under Spanish rule, native Andean weaving underwent a transformation through the introduction of new materials (linen, sheep's wool, metal-wrapped threads from Europe, and silk from China), new ideas (European artistic conventions and Asian textile designs), and new uses (domestic objects such as carpets, cushions, and covers, instead of traditional Andean garments).

Despite the changes they forced upon native Andean weavers, the Spanish did not completely extinguish the tradition of elite Inca textile manufacture. Native artisans continued to make fine tapestry-woven garments, essential signifiers of social identity in preconquest Inca culture, during the colonial period. The mantle shown here is one superb example of the survival of high-status Inca textiles. Woven in two sections in the labor-intensive interlocked tapestry technique, it contains over seventy-eight wefts per centimeter in places, a feat of technical virtuosity associated with elite Inca fabrics. Yet it also includes a cotton warp, indicating a likely colonial-period manufacture. The quality of the weaving and the unusual patterns suggest that the mantle perhaps was created as a burial shroud for a descendent of Inca nobility.

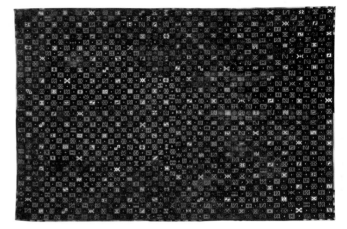

Mantle or shroud

Peru

Late Inca / early colonial period, about 1550

Wool and cotton interlocked tapestry with overstitched edging

119 x 171 cm (46¾ x 67⅜ in.)

Charles Potter Kling Fund 1988.325

The mantle's design features an extraordinary overall pattern of 1,824 small geometric motifs known as *tocapu*. In preconquest Inca society, *tocapu* were reserved for the very highest rank of society and often appeared on tunics in bands. The unusually small size of these *tocapu* and their carefully planned arrangement on the shroud suggest a later transitional style. The mantle may have had an additional function: when divided into five equal sections, it creates a five-year calendar, a classic Andean temporal organization.

Far more typical of colonial-period textiles was a hybrid style that combined European-influenced design elements with Andean weaving techniques. European inspiration came in many forms, from the decorative arts brought by the Spanish to the New World (including ceramics, silver, furniture, tapestries, carpets, lace, and embroidered textiles and clothing) to paintings, sculptures, and the more readily collectible prints. The tapestry at right, possibly a table cover, illustrates this range of influences.

Four symmetrical borders surround a central field. European-style scrolling flowers and strapwork within the bands of the border relate to decorative elements in contemporary embroidery. At the axis of the main field, two baskets containing flowers feature a checkerboard pattern reminiscent of traditional Andean design. Further European influence can be seen in the parrots and the urns filled with floral bouquets typical of popular taste in European paintings and decorative arts of the late seventeenth and eigh-

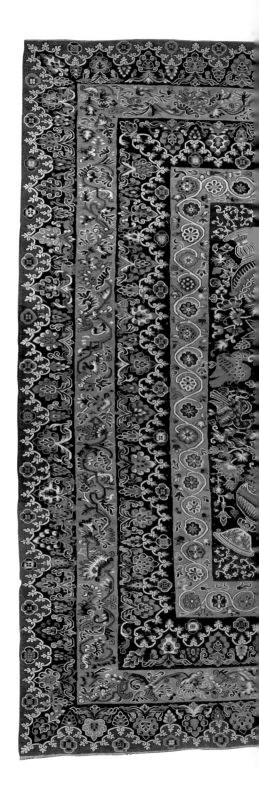

Cover

Peru

Colonial period, mid-18th century or later

Wool and cotton interlocked and

dovetailed tapestry with eccentric wefts

243.4 x 213 cm (95¾ x 83¾ in.)

Denman Waldo Ross Collection   04.1619

teenth centuries. The figures depicted in cartouches, representing a Hungarian, a Turk, a Frenchman, and a German, derive from engravings by the French artist Jacques Callot that were first published in 1622 and remained popular well into the eighteenth century.

Another profound influence on Andean weavers came from China. Trading ships known as the "Manila galleons" brought desirable Chinese goods, such as tea and silk embroideries and tapestries, over the Pacific Ocean from the Philippines, another Spanish colony, to the official New World port at Acapulco. From there, the wares were transshipped over land to the port of Veracruz and shipped to Spain. Many galleons ventured south to Peru, where resident colonials appreciated the valuable silks. The tapestry at right, created by native artisans, reveals many Asian-inspired motifs and was woven with silk thread, another precious commodity gained from Pacific trade. Dispersed throughout the borders and central field of the cover are large-scale peonies and phoenixes. Most notable is the inclusion of the *xeizai*, a mythical Chinese creature with a single horn and a lionlike body. The red background likely reflects Chinese taste and the concept of "yang," or happiness. Interspersed among the obvious Asian motifs are clearly European-influenced elements including dogs, deer, and crowned lions. Native Andean animals—llamas and viscacha—also appear in the outermost decorative border, rendering this tapestry a melting pot of three cultures.

LDW

Cover

Peru

Colonial period, late 17th–early 18th
century

Wool, silk, cotton, and linen interlocked and dovetailed tapestry

238.3 x 207.3 cm (93 ¾ x 81½ in.)

Denman Waldo Ross Collection

11.1264

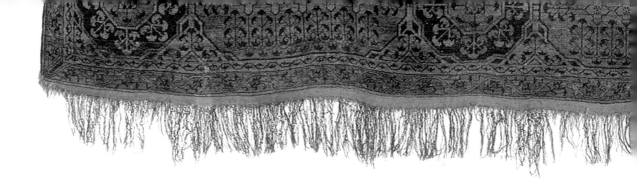

Early Islamic Court Carpets

The large and diverse group of textiles usually referred to as "oriental carpets" encompasses carpets made over many centuries across a geographic area stretching from China to North Africa. The designs of these carpets vary widely, from traditional geometric motifs that a tribal weaver could learn to knot from memory, to complex curvilinear and pictorial designs created in advance by artists and woven in professional workshops. Of the second category, the finest and most influential on later designs were the carpets woven for the great Islamic courts of the sixteenth century. The rulers of the Mamluk dynasty in Egypt, the Safavid dynasty in Persia, and the Mughal dynasty in India all gave high priority to the weaving of fine carpets, which they laid on the floors of palaces and shrines, spread on the ground in royal tent encampments, and gave as precious diplomatic gifts.

Mamluk carpets made in Egypt in the fifteenth and sixteenth centuries are unique in their complex geometric designs and limited color palette. Much about their origins and production remains mysterious. Their designs incorporate some elements found in contemporary Anatolian and Spanish carpets, and their pile is knotted with the same asymmetric knot used in Persia. However, their creators also drew motifs from Mamluk metalwork and architectural ornament, Coptic tapestry, and native Egyptian plant imagery. The weavers may have developed these intricate and distinctive designs, as well as the unusual red, green, and blue color scheme, in a conscious attempt to distinguish their work from carpets made elsewhere. The European export market was extremely lucrative, and many Mamluk carpets were exported to Europe. There, they were often used as table covers, which may explain the roughly square proportions of many of the surviving examples.

Carpet

Egypt (probably Cairo)

Mamluk dynasty, mid-16th century

Wool warp and weft with wool knotted pile

278.9 x 268.9 cm (109 13/16 x 105 7/8 in.)

Helen and Alice Colburn Fund and Harriet Otis Cruft Fund   61.939

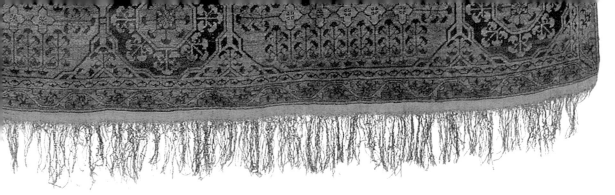

In the early sixteenth century, under the patronage of the Safavid rulers, the arts of miniature painting, manuscript illumination, and bookbinding flourished in Persia. The design of carpets and textiles soon reflected the influence of the court painters, who probably drew cartoons for some of the lively figural images of battling animals and royal hunts that appear on Safavid carpets and velvets. The masterful example above most likely was woven in the royal workshops of, or as a commission from, Shah Tahmasp I. Two of Tahmasp's greatest court artists, Aqa Mirak and Sultan Muhammad, may have designed it. The use of expensive silk, the addition of precious-metal-

wrapped threads in some areas, and the extremely fine craftsmanship all suggest its royal quality.

The carpet's composition may also point to its royal associations. Scenes of hunting, a popular courtly pastime that became a recurring theme in all Persian art, occupy the main field. The border, with its images of elegant courtiers feasting in a garden, would appear right-side up only to someone (presumably the Shah) seated on a dais at the center of the carpet, whereas the hunters subduing their prey, perhaps symbolizing royal power, would be right-side up to both the Shah and his audience.

In India, the sixteenth-century Mughal emperor

Hunting carpet
Probably designed by Aqa Mirak and
Sultan Muhammad for Shah Tahmasp I
Iran
Safavid dynasty, about 1530
Silk warp and weft with silk knotted pile, with
supplementary metal-wrapped patterning wefts
480.1 x 225 cm (189 x 88⁹⁄₁₆ in.)
Centennial Purchase Fund, Gift of John Goelet,
and unrestricted textile purchase funds 66.293

Akbar is credited with establishing the first royal workshop for weaving pile carpets, which previously were uncommon there. Emigré artists from Persia likely made the earliest Mughal carpets, which show a strong Persian influence. However, distinctively Indian designs, including compositions of grotesque animals devouring each other, soon emerged. Also, as in Safavid Persia, a close relationship developed between painting and carpet design. This connection is evident in the pictorial carpet illustrated on page 72, one of the most famous of all Mughal rugs.

Within a border of palmettes and grotesque masks, the center field of this beautifully preserved carpet fol-lows the format of a manuscript page. Three distinct vignettes are set among naturalistically rendered plants and animals. At the top is a scene of palace life, with two men conversing in a pavilion, fanned by a servant. Part of a noble hunting party, including an oxcart with a tethered cheetah, crosses the center of the carpet. The vignette at the bottom shows a half-lion, half-elephant creature from Indian mythology demonstrating its strength by holding seven elephants, while being attacked by a mythical bird whose origin may be Persian, or even Chinese.

SW

Ottoman Textiles

Ottoman textiles from the fifteenth through seventeenth centuries are some of the most sumptuous cloths ever produced. Admired for their bold and exotic designs, these luxurious fabrics reflect the power and glory of the Ottoman Empire, which at its height spanned three continents—Europe, Asia, and Africa.

Centered at the crossroads of Europe and Asia in Turkey, the Ottoman state had grown wealthy as a pivotal trading depot by the fifteenth century. It also had become a melting pot for artistic ideas. Weavers in the court manufactories at the Ottoman cities of Bursa and Istanbul, where the famed Silk Road and the Mediterranean maritime routes converged, were influenced by goods going both east and west, especially the rich velvets produced in the Italian city-states of Genoa and Florence and the sophisticated figured silks created in the Safavid court of Persia.

By the mid-sixteenth-century reign of Sultan Süleyman the Magnificent, however, a distinctly Ottoman aesthetic began to emerge, characterized by a standard repertoire of patterns; a boldness of line, color, and scale; and a quality of sober grandeur. The Ottoman court preferred three types of fabrics, which reflected the rising Ottoman style: figured silk, or *kemha*; velvet, known as *kadife* or *çatma*; and cloth of gold or silver, called *seraser*. The court used these fabrics lavishly as high-status garments and furnishing fabrics. Rulers also bestowed them as important diplomatic gifts, thus transmitting the splendor of the Ottoman court abroad.

Artisans produced *kemha* in great quantity, creating rich, colorful patterns often embellished with metal-wrapped threads. Within the standardized floral vocabulary of Ottoman design, *kemha* reflected substantial creativity and experimentation with pattern. The panel illustrated here features many of the elements common to Ottoman *kemha* of the late sixteenth century. The overall design is organized into staggered ogival medallions, one of the most popular pattern layouts. It is woven in crimson, blue, white, and pistachio silk yarns with metal-wrapped threads in a typical weave structure known as a lampas, which in this case combines a satin ground weave with a twill pattern weave. Images of tulips, carnations, and roses unite with graceful, serrated petals associated with an earlier decorative mode known as the Saz style to produce an exuberant and elegant kaftan fabric.

Velvet, or *kadife*, weaving probably originated in Italy and spread in the fifteenth century to Turkey, where it became a specialty of the manufactories at Bursa for cushion covers as well as garments. Figured velvets brocaded with precious metals required silk

Length of velvet
Turkey
Ottoman dynasty, first half of 16th century
Silk cut and voided velvet with supplementary
metal-wrapped patterning wefts
69 x 64 cm (27⅛ x 25⅛ in.)
Denman Waldo Ross Collection 04.121

pile warps as much as fifteen times longer than the finished fabric and were a particular marker of status. The velvet needed for a single kaftan might take six months to weave. The fragment shown at right illustrates the opulence associated with Ottoman velvets and displays a *çintamani* (auspicious jewel) pattern, one of the most recognizable and enduring of Ottoman designs. The *çintamani* design, comprised of three circles or balls and two wavy lines, derives originally from Buddhist symbols. However, the Ottomans associated the *çintamani* with the garb of Rustam, the warrior hero of Persian poetry, and with the spots and stripes of leopard and tiger skins. This fragment probably was part of a kaftan. With its connotations of masculinity, prowess, and good luck, the bold and sumptuous velvet *çintamani* would have proclaimed its wearer's rank and status, even when seen from a distance.

Seraser, known in the West as "cloth of gold or silver," was the costliest and most prestigious of all Ottoman fabrics. Its surface was entirely covered with silver- and gold-wrapped weft threads. Documents suggest that tradition reserved *seraser* for the highest-ranking members of the imperial household and often limited it to kaftans worn at ceremonial occasions. However, these sumptuary restrictions seem to have proven ineffectual; the number of looms weaving *seraser* gradually increased, providing this luxury fabric to a widening market.

Artisans in the imperial weaving workshops of Istanbul probably made the early example of *seraser* weaving seen at far right. Woven in taqueté, an ancient weave structure typical of *seraser*, the textile boasts both silver and gilt silver weft threads across its surface. It depicts a stylized peacock-feather pattern that was one of the most popular Ottoman motifs and was associated with Islamic legends of the Garden of Eden. The artist rendered the three-lobed peacock feather in large scale, boldly outlining it with pistachio-colored silk yarns in an excellent variation on this pattern.

LDW

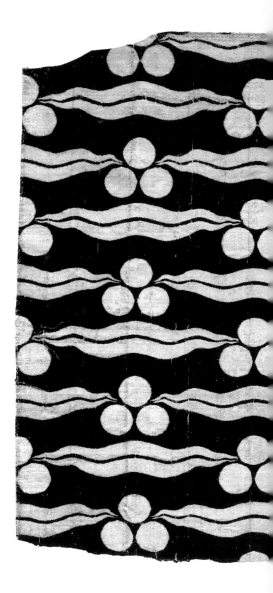

Panel from a garment
Turkey
Ottoman dynasty, first half of 17th century
Silk and metal-wrapped thread
compound weft plain weave (taqueté)
129 x 55 cm (50¾ x 21⅝ in.)
Denman Waldo Ross Collection   08.387

Panel from a garment

Turkey

Ottoman dynasty, 1575–85

Silk lampas with supplementary metal-
wrapped patterning wefts

106 x 55 cm (41¾ x 21½ in.)

Denman Waldo Ross Collection   06.359

Elizabethan Embroidery

The first great flowering of English embroidery occurred in the thirteenth and fourteenth centuries, when ecclesiastical vestments and altar frontals known as *opus Anglicanum*, embroidered in professional English workshops, became renowned throughout Europe. The Protestant Reformation, which in England began when King Henry VIII severed ties with the Roman Catholic Church in 1534, put an end to this industry. However, the reign of Henry's daughter, Queen Elizabeth I, ushered in a new golden age for artistic achievement, this time in the sphere of secular and domestic embroidery.

Professional embroiderers, who were noted for their skill in working with difficult materials such as metal threads, wire, and precious stones, turned their attention to creating elaborate gowns, masque costumes, and pageant attire for Elizabeth's court. They also produced many smaller luxury items such as decorated book bindings, bags, and gloves. The pair of gloves illustrated here undoubtedly was made by a professional embroiderer, whose mastery is evident in the many kinds of metal threads and wire employed and in the expert manipulation of materials to create rich surface textures and three-dimensional effects. Fine gloves such as these, featuring elaborately decorated cuffs and often perfumed, were fashionable accessories and status symbols for both men and women. They were also considered tokens of loyalty and fidelity, and were commonly exchanged as gifts.

A new phenomenon developed in the sixteenth century: the skilled amateur embroiderer. The number of prosperous households in England greatly increased, and families expressed their new wealth largely by building and furnishing houses. Richly decorated textiles such as bed hangings and cushion covers, which provided comfort and warmth and also displayed the owners' wealth and taste, frequently were the most important and expensive component of a house's furnishings. Well-to-do ladies increasingly were inspired to embroider such items for themselves, and skill in needlework became one of the necessary accomplishments of a cultured woman. Girls were instructed in embroidery from an early age, and many became so proficient that it is often difficult to distinguish between amateur and professional work.

Embroiderers found design ideas in printed pattern books, which began to proliferate in the early seventeenth century, and in prints and illustrated books showing scenes from the Bible and classical literature. On one cushion cover (pp. 80–81), Apollo with his bow is shown pursuing the nymph Daphne, who is transforming into a laurel tree to escape him. The

Pair of gloves
England
Early 17th century
Leather embroidered with silk, seed pearls, metallic threads, and spangles, and trimmed with metallic bobbin lace, woven silk, and metallic ribbon
a: 36 x 20 cm (14 3/16 x 7 7/8 in.), b: 35.5 x 20 cm (14 x 7 7/8 in.)
Gift of Philip Lehman in memory of his wife Carrie L. Lehman
38.1351a–b

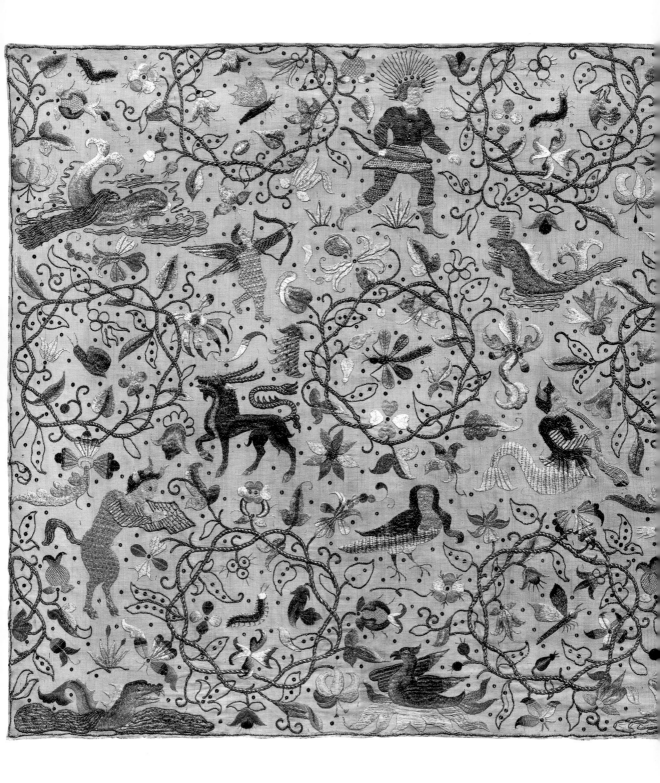

Cushion cover
England
1600–1650
Linen plain weave, embroidered
with silk and metallic threads,
peacock feathers, and spangles
58.4 x 93 cm (23 x 36⅝ in.)
The Elizabeth Day McCormick Collection
43.406

artist most likely copied these figures, along with several of the other gods and mythological creatures, from an illustrated edition of Ovid's *Metamorphoses*. Insects, snails, and butterflies were popular motifs for embroidery, and the maker may have selected those seen here from a pattern book. Many families relied upon professional draftsmen to draw patterns on fabric for the women of the house to embroider, and the balanced composition and freely drawn roundels of flowering vines on the cushion cover suggest that its maker probably employed such a professional to prepare her pattern.

The English love of flowers and gardening found expression in the popularity of floral designs of all kinds. Embroiderers commonly depicted floral "slips," so-called because they resembled the slips, or cuttings, that gardeners use for grafting or propagation. These motifs derived from the botanical illustrations in books called herbals, which listed the medicinal and other properties of various plants. On this cover, possibly used on a table or bench, floral slips appear in a stylized form. The designer arranged the individual flowers, including roses, cornflowers, carnations, and irises, in a lattice of wavy lines to form a rich and lively overall pattern.

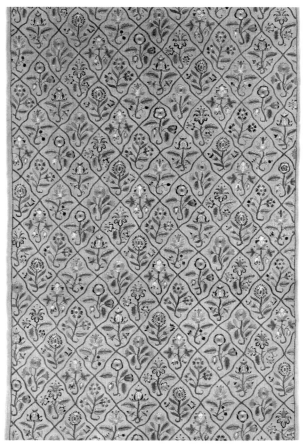

Part of a long cover
England
Early 17th century
Linen plain weave, embroidered
with silk and metallic threads
186.1 x 77.2 cm (73 1/4 x 30 3/8 in.)
The Elizabeth Day McCormick Collection   43.253

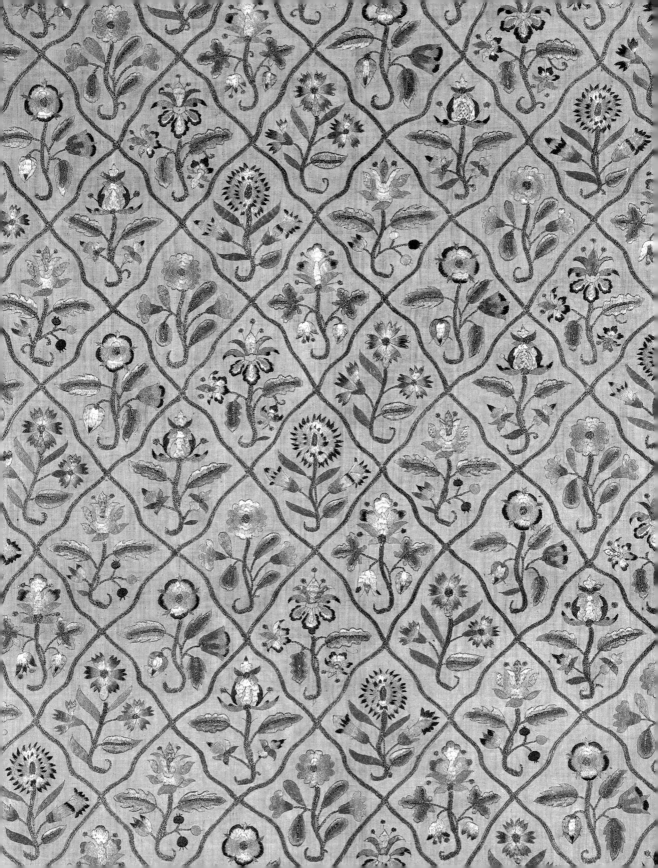

Woman's jacket

England

About 1610–15, with later alterations

Linen plain weave, embroidered with silk, metallic threads, and spangles, and trimmed with metallic bobbin lace

Center back length: 43 cm (16¹⁵⁄₁₆ in.)

The Elizabeth Day McCormick Collection 43.243

Meandering floral vines with coiling tendrils provided another popular and characteristically English design. Embroiderers often used this type of design on costume items such as men's informal caps and women's coifs, or headdresses. Women's jackets completely embroidered in this kind of pattern, such as this example decorated with daffodils, were fashionable from about 1550 to 1650. This jacket and a matching coif and triangular forehead cloth were made about 1610–15 and are unusual in being embroidered entirely with expensive gold and silver threads. The jacket was altered to a more fashionable shape in about 1630 and is in remarkably fresh and untarnished condition.

SW

Flowers of Mughal India

India has been famous as a source for luxury textiles, particularly fine cottons, since ancient times. Under the rule of the Mughal dynasty, however, India's textile artisans achieved new heights in design and craftsmanship. Beginning with Emperor Akbar in the sixteenth century, the Mughal rulers took a particular interest in textiles, establishing royal workshops for all kinds of weaving, embroidery, printing, and dyeing, and made efforts to improve the quality of existing industries. Luxurious textiles dressed the Mughal court and provided much of the furnishings and decoration of its palaces and tent encampments, which astonished contemporary visitors with their splendor.

A characteristic feature of Mughal design is the decorative use of single, naturalistically drawn flowering plants. Artists most likely adapted these plant motifs from the illustrations in European botanical books, which the Mughal emperors avidly collected. Floral motifs were more widely adopted during the reign of Emperor Jahangir, who visited the northern territory of Kashmir in the spring of 1620 and was so captivated by the abundant flowers that he instructed his artists to capture their beauty in detailed paintings.

Textiles patterned with flowering plants decorated the interiors of most Mughal royal palaces and tents, and floral carpets created the illusion of beautiful meadows underfoot. Floor coverings were an essential part of the furnishings of any royal chamber, because most functions of daily life were carried out while seated on the floor. In hot and humid weather, cotton floor spreads, or "summer carpets," covered or replaced the customary pile carpets of wool or silk.

With its design of poppy plants in staggered rows, the floor spread fragment on page 86 at first appears quite simple. A guest seated upon it, however, would appreciate its clear colors and fine details, achieved through a complex process of stenciling, painting, and successive applications of dyes, wax resist, and other chemical agents.

The shawl-weaving industry in Kashmir also attracted the attention of the Mughal emperors, and with their encouragement it began to flourish in the mid-seventeenth century. Individual flowering plants set against plain backgrounds, in the manner favored by Emperor Jahangir, decorate the *pallu*, or end panels, of the earliest surviving Kashmir shawls, such as the example illustrated on page 87. The most luxurious of these early shawls were made of fine goat hair, called *pashmina*. Their makers wove them so skillfully that the patterned areas, made by interlocking yarns of many colors in a tapestry weave, are as light and supple as the plain areas.

Male courtiers wore sashes called *patka*, which they wrapped several times around their coats, with the decorated ends hanging loose in front. Most *patka*, whether woven, printed, painted, or embroidered, were decorated with flowering plants, following the fashion of the Mughal court. By the end of the seventeenth century, the flowering plant motifs on shawls and sashes had become more stylized and complex. The makers of the splendid woven sash on page 88, for example, transformed the poppylike plants into dense bushes, with miniature peacocks and other birds perched in their branches.

Shawl (detail)
India (Kashmir)
Mughal dynasty, mid-17th century
Fine goat hair (*pashmina*) interlocked
twill tapestry
241 x 126 cm (94 7/8 x 49 5/8 in.)
Anonymous gift in the name of Mrs. Arthur T. Ca
45.540

Fragment of a floor spread
India (possibly Burhanpur, the Deccan)
Mughal dynasty, late 17th or early 18th century
Cotton plain weave, painted,
mordant dyed, and resist dyed
164.5 x 111.1 cm (64 3/4 x 43 3/4 in.)
Gift of John Goelet 66.866

Patka (sash)

India

Mughal dynasty, 17th or early 18th century

Silk twill with supplementary silk and

metal-wrapped patterning wefts

330 x 52.1 cm (129 15/16 x 20 1/2 in.)

Gift of John Goelet 66.858

Patka (sash)
India (Golconda or Burhanpur, the Deccan)
Mughal dynasty, early 18th century
Cotton plain weave, printed, painted,
mordant dyed, and resist dyed, with
metal-wrapped thread fringe
67 x 525.8 cm (26⅜ x 207 in.)
Gift of John Goelet   66.859

An elegant printed and painted *patka* of roughly the same date (above) shows the next step in the evolution of the flowering plant motif. The delicate, treelike plants with chrysanthemum blossoms lean slightly to the left and have begun to transmute into the abstract, teardrop-shaped *boteh* motif—known in the West as the paisley pattern—that developed over the course of the eighteenth century. This *patka* also exemplifies the beauty and technical refinement of Indian printed and painted cottons, called chintzes, which were highly prized in Europe as well as India.

SW

Chinese Dragon Robes

The dragon has many meanings in China. He reigns as the king of the beasts and is known as a protector, as the herald of spring, and as an emblem of the principle *yang*, or maleness and creation. A powerful symbol of China itself, he found his way onto most of the textiles and clothing associated with the emperor, his courtiers, and his officials. Men of the court wore lavish robes embroidered and woven with dragons as early as the Tang dynasty (618–907), and the tradition continued and flourished during the Ming (1368–1644) and Qing (1644–1911) eras.

Confucian beliefs held that it was the duty of the Chinese emperor to wear silk in order to distinguish himself from his subjects and help maintain the hierarchy. The emperor also embodied *li*, or virtue, and needed garments that made him easily recognizable so others could learn from his behavior. Based on these Confucian beliefs, Chinese court dress developed into an important expression of rank and imperial favor, not only for the emperor but for his family, the nobility, and military and civil officials as well. Regulations set down and modified over the centuries governed who was allowed to wear which color or hat ornament and who could display five-clawed, rather than four-clawed, dragons on their robes.

Lavishly embellished robes also served as important diplomatic gifts. The emperor bestowed robes on visiting dignitaries, neighboring rulers, and (to keep them at bay) marauding nomads from the north. This example probably went to Tibet, with whom the Chinese maintained close diplomatic and economic ties, as just such a gift. The large forward-facing dragon portrayed on the robe has a third eye. This symbol of inward vision is associated with esoteric Buddhism practiced in Tibet and fashionable in China during the

Man's robe restyled as a Tibetan *chuba*

China (found in Tibet)
Late Ming / early Qing dynasty, 17th century
Silk, metal-wrapped, and peacock-feather-wrapped
thread slit tapestry
Center back length: 146.7 cm (57¾ in.)
Museum purchase with funds donated anonymously   2001.145

early Qing dynasty. The large scale of the dragon and his animated facial expression are typical of Ming-dynasty and very early Qing-dynasty robes. The robe was later restyled as a Tibetan garment known as a *chuba*. However, the original Chinese cut did not differ greatly, and we can still appreciate the configuration of the design in its current tailoring, which places dragons at the four cardinal points—front, back, and shoulders—against clouds, with mountains rising out of water below.

These design elements became standardized in the eighteenth century. Another robe (above) shows the format that developed during the first half of the century. Nine dragons now appear—one each at the front, back, and shoulders, two at the bottom front, two at the bottom back, and one hiding beneath the front flap. The bottom border has increased in size and shows more impressive waves.

The Qianlong emperor codified the decorative scheme of the dragon robe, or *long pao*, in 1759 when he issued the *Illustrated Precedents for the Ritual Paraphernalia of the Imperial Court*. The symbolism of the robe was still closely aligned with Confucian ideals, with which the eighteenth-century emperors directly identified. The *long pao* served as a model of the universe with the emperor at its center. Known as *lishui*, the wavelike border at the bottom represented the universal ocean surrounding the earth. Mountain peaks rising from the waves at the center front, back, and sides of the robe symbolized the four cardinal points, and the nine dragons residing in a cloud-filled sky above signified imperial authority. However, the symbolism was only complete when the robe was worn. The wearer's body became the central axis that aligned the forces of earth with heaven.

As the Qing dynasty continued, the dragon robe changed subtly: the *lishui* increased in size as the scale of the dragons decreased. The example above, from the last quarter of the eighteenth century, shows the evolution. The robe's blue silk background is completely patterned in metal-wrapped yarns. Artists made many robes in this style, decorating the less costly examples with gold-colored silk. How the court used the robes is, unfortunately, unknown. *Long pao* of the nineteenth century show similar trends, although the quality of the robes declined along with the empire itself. When the Qing dynasty came to a close in 1912, dragon robes became a symbol of the imperial past and were outlawed throughout China. The Mao suit replaced them as the new sartorial symbol of political allegiance.

PAP

Man's robe (*long pao*) (above)
China
Qing dynasty, fourth quarter of the 18th century
Silk plain weave with supplementary silk and metal-wrapped patterning wefts
45.4 x 198 cm (57¼ x 78 in.)
Gift of Marco Pallis   50.744

Man's robe (*long pao*) (left)
China
Qing dynasty, first quarter of the 18th century
Silk satin with supplementary continuous and discontinuous silk and gold-wrapped patterning wefts
139.5 x 206 cm (55 x 81 in.)
The James Fund   02.49

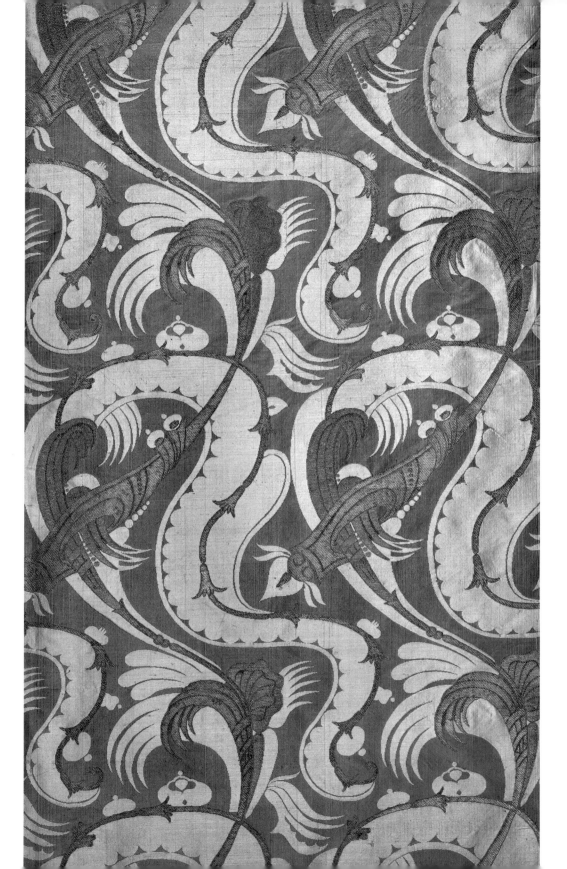

Early Eighteenth-Century European Silks

Louis XIV and his finance minister Jean-Baptiste Colbert emphasized the development of the luxury textile trades in France during the seventeenth century in an attempt to stem the flow of French francs to Italy, Flanders, and other important textile centers of the time. The French lace-making and silk, ribbon, and passementerie weaving trades flourished as a result, as did spinning, dyeing, and finishing. When Louis revoked the Edict of Nantes in 1685, eradicating the rights of French Protestants, many weavers and other skilled craftsmen of the Protestant faith left France for England and Holland and strengthened the textile industries in those countries. By the end of the century, northern European silk industries had grown unprecedentedly. An explosion of innovative and exuberant textile designs set the stage for a most exciting period in the history of European silk weaving.

One of the earliest and most original styles of eighteenth-century textile design flourished about 1700. Silks designed in this style are now known as "bizarre" silks, owing to the title of a book by an early researcher of these fabrics, Heinrich Sloman. Large repeats and flowing, complex designs that defy characterization distinguish the fabrics. The inspirations for these designs remain a mystery; two possible sources are Asia—China, Japan, India, or Indonesia—and the microscopic world of biology that had just become visible due to the discoveries of the Dutch scientist Anton van Leeuwenhoek. Two large panels sewn together (seen at left) illustrate this style. The repeat is forty-seven centimeters long and recurs twice along the tex-

fig. 13 **The fabric design on these 1991 shoes by Vivian Westwood was inspired by the MFA's eighteenth-century silk damask.**

Two textile lengths, stitched together (detail)

France or Holland

About 1700

Silk damask with supplementary silk and metal-wrapped patterning wefts

244 x 113 cm (96¼ x 43 in.)

Textile Income Purchase Fund   1977.179

tile's width. Large undulating amoeba-like forms pattern the bicolor damask, bringing to mind the life seen under a microscope or the designs created on Javanese batiks. Further patterns brocaded into the textile can only be described as space-age, plantlike forms.

The influence of Asia is more obvious on other textiles such as the Dutch silk used to make the dress illustrated below. Here exotic, "oriental" landscapes and seascapes float against a satin ground. The fabric, which was probably woven in Amsterdam, was known during the early eighteenth-century as an *Indienne*— an acknowledgement of its design sources, although it is more Chinese than Indian. This is typical of how designers of the seventeenth and eighteenth centuries understood and translated their impressions of the East into their work, mixing and melding Chinese, Japanese, and Indian motifs.

The complexity, beauty, and expense of early eighteenth-century textiles greatly influenced the design of clothing during the period, especially women's dresses. As fabric patterns became more elaborate, the skirts of women's dresses seem to have expanded in size to act as a better framework on which to display the silk designers' art. The rare survival of a dress that has not been restyled since it was made about 1730

Dress, petticoat, and stomacher
Fabric made in Holland
About 1735; dress restyled at a later date
Silk satin with supplementary discontinuous
silk and metal-wrapped patterning wefts
Center back length: overdress 160 cm (63 in.);
center front length: stomacher and petticoat (now attached)
112 x 100.3 cm (44 ½ x 39 ½ in.)
The Elizabeth Day McCormick Collection   43.1871a–c

(below) illustrates how the cut and construction of clothing was subservient to the textiles out of which it was fashioned.

Most eighteenth-century dresses actually comprise two parts, a petticoat and an overdress that opened down the front to expose the underskirt beneath. A seamstress would stitch together four to six lengths of fabric and pleat or gather them at the top to construct a petticoat. The maker of this gown's petticoat used four lengths. Another four lengths of fabric, two at the back and two at the front, compose the overdress. The seamstress fit the back of the dress by double-box pleating each panel at the top, and shaped the front by pleating along each side of the center front of the bodice. Sleeves are the only tailored part of a dress in this style, which was known as a *robe volante* in France and a *sacque* in England. The method of constructing the overdress prevented the dressmaker from cutting away too much of the valuable fabric and meant that as styles changed, the dress could easily be taken apart and remade. This gown's fabric is typical of the 1730s and 1740s, when more naturalistic designs became fashionable. The wide skirts, often worn under a pannier, or hoop, created a perfect surface on which to show off the design of the textile.

PAP

Dress and petticoat
France
About 1730
Silk lampas
Center back length: overdress 152.5 cm (60 in.),
petticoat 97 cm (38¼ in.)
The Elizabeth Day McCormick Collection   43.664a–b

Colonial Boston Embroidery

In colonial Boston, one of a woman's most important and often enjoyable tasks was plying the needle. At an early age girls were trained in the needle arts, both plain and fancy. Plain work refers to basic stitching techniques that women employed to make linens, chemises, and shirts for the household. Fancy work refers to decorative stitches that ornamented the textiles and clothing used in daily life, such as bed hangings, petticoat borders, and chair covers. The MFA's collection of colonial Boston embroidery, one of the country's finest, provides a colorful picture of the colonial Boston home.

A colonial home's most valuable furnishings were its bed hangings. The textiles and embroidery yarns needed to create the curtains, valances, counterpane, and head cloth implied a high level of household income. That a woman of the house could take time away from chores to embroider them also was a sign of luxury. A member of the Bradstreet family of Boston reportedly worked this bed-curtain. The undulating floral stems take their inspiration from English designs of the late seventeenth century that were either brought to the new world with the colonists or imported at a later date. Large, dense foliate vines growing out of a landscape below characterize the English patterns. By the early eighteenth century, as such designs passed out of fashion, more naturalistic ones took their place. Although the pattern for the Bradstreet hangings may have been imported from England, it might in fact have been drawn locally in Boston, as it is consistent with the lighter, more delicate designs that characterize other examples from the city.

Wide bed-curtain
Possibly made by a member of the Bradstreet family
New England colonies (Boston)
1725–50
Cotton and linen plain weave, embroidered with wool
219.5 x 190 cm (86½ x 74¾ in.)
Gift of Samuel Bradstreet   19.67

Embroidered picture
Ann Peartree (about 1722–1744)
New England colonies (Boston)
1739
Linen plain weave, embroidered with wool and silk
27.7 x 23 cm (10⅞ x 9 in.)
Bequest of Elsie T. Friedman 59.22

Historical records indicate that a number of women who taught embroidery also drew patterns. Both women and men diversified their income-earning activities to support themselves in the growing New England economy. An advertisement published in the *Boston Gazette* indicates that Susanna Condy sold patterns for pocketbooks, screens, housewifes (small containers for sewing equipment), and chimneypieces. In addition to drawing patterns, Mrs. Condy offered for sale a set of bed-curtains that she had worked from a London pattern. However, her most consistent income came from teaching young girls the stitching skills necessary for plain and fancy work.

A schoolgirl's first project was the creation of a sampler, in which she worked the alphabet, numbers, and simple patterned bands in cross-stitch and other useful stitches. The style of sampler most identified with Boston, specifically the North End, includes embroidered pictures of Adam and Eve at the bottom. Researchers have attributed this type to Mrs. Condy's school, but it probably was shared by a number of women teaching in the North End. After a sampler, many girls completed canvas-work pictures. This kind of work was especially popular during the mid-eighteenth century. Ann Peartree worked the earliest dated Boston schoolgirl picture, seen here. It features a personification of Spring sitting in a landscape. At the bottom, Ann embroidered her name and the year 1739. The picture is now faded, but the back still shows how colorful and vibrant it must have been.

fig. 14 The reverse of Ann Peartree's
picture shows the original colors of
the embroidery.

The most famous pictures Boston schoolgirls embroidered are overmantels, or chimneypieces. The majority of these overmantels depict pastoral scenes inspired by printed sources. One of the most well-known is this piece that Eunice Bourne, of Barnstable, Massachusetts, embroidered midcentury when she attended school in Boston. The overmantel contains three scenes: a woman spinning, a couple strolling through a landscape, and, in the center, a woman fishing. This central scene gave these embroideries their nickname: "fishing lady" pictures. Many such pieces worked by Boston schoolgirls are beautifully framed and would have hung proudly in the family home.

Embroidered overmantel with original frame

Eunice Bourne (born in 1732, died between
1773 and 1781)
New England colonies (Boston)
1745–50
Linen plain weave, embroidered with wool, silk,
metal-wrapped thread, and glass beads
63 x 129 cm (24¾ x 50¾ in.)
Seth K. Sweetser Fund   21.2233

The samplers, embroidered pictures, furnishings, and clothing not only tell a story of female education and economy but also illustrate the continuity of design that existed in eighteenth-century Boston. A case in point is a later sampler made by Sally Jackson in 1771. By the end of the eighteenth century, samplers became more pictorial than practical, and this example, with its elaborate floral border, represents one of the most attractive of the late-century styles. Nevertheless, it shows the influence of previous Boston designs, particularly in the landscape scene at the bottom, which has precedents in earlier work. The Bourne overmantel, for example, contains similar imagery, including the parrot in the tree and the leaping stag. However, one of the most direct comparisons is with a mid-eighteenth-century petticoat border that contains an almost identical scene. The person who drew the sampler's design probably took inspiration from an earlier work or a style she learned from her mother or embroidery instructress, who in turn was influenced by the patterns that arrived from London in the early eighteenth century.

PAP

fig. 15 **A leaping stag and a tree containing an oversize parrot comprise a scene often found on colonial embroidery, as on this mid-eighteenth-century petticoat border.**

Sampler

Sally Jackson (born in 1760)
New England colonies (Boston)
1771
Linen plain weave, embroidered with silk
76.2 x 50.8 cm (30 x 20 in.)
Museum purchase with funds donated anonymously and Frank B. Bemis Fund
2001.739

ABCDEF GHKLMNOPQRS
TVWXYZ 12345678

From My Beginning May The
Almighty Powers Blessings Bestow
In Never Ceasing Showers May
Plenty Dissipate All Worldly Care
And Smiling Peace Bless My
Revolving Years

Sally Jackson Her Sampler 1771

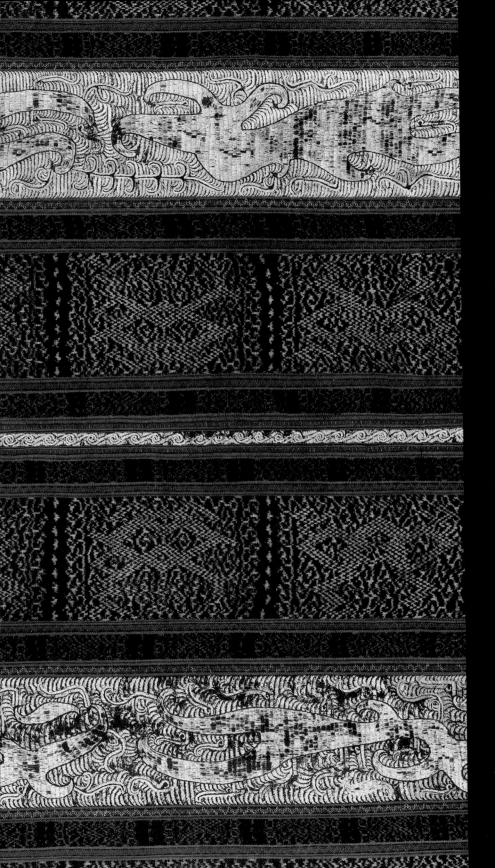

Tradition and Industry 1750–1875

The eighteenth century was a period of great technical innovation, especially in the textile fields. Textile spinning methods were mechanized, roller printing developed, and knitting and lace machines invented. By 1805 the French inventor Joseph Marie Jacquard introduced his mechanized patterning device, which revolutionized weaving and eventually led to the development of the computer. All of this experimentation paved the way for the Industrial Revolution, which was led by the textile industries. The new mechanized production methods greatly reduced the expense and time needed to produce textiles. Patterned cloth and quality wools were now more widely available and affordable. The greater accessibility of fine cloth for making men's suits contributed to blurring the lines between the social classes and helped facilitate the economic democratization of the nineteenth century.

The Industrial Revolution also affected less-developed nations who traded with the West. Although they preserved their traditional textile methods longer, these nations incorporated new materials, techniques, and designs into their work. Such influences can be seen in the raffia cloth made by the Kuba people of the Congo, who learned embroidery stitches from missionaries, and in the rich textiles of the Minangkabau in Sumatra, who relished the silk and gold-wrapped thread acquired through trade. Western manufactured goods also found their way to these countries and, because they could be made so cheaply, began to replace traditional textiles throughout the world. By the end of the nineteenth century, the textile and apparel trades had mechanized so completely that it is now difficult for us to imagine the high value and preciousness of textiles produced prior to the Industrial Revolution.

fig. 16 Shortly after Japan opened to the West in 1858, it began importing labor-saving devices such as the sewing machine.

The Fashionable Fan

While fans historically served practical functions such as cooling the air or stirring up fires, they performed a decorative one as well. They have been important fashionable accessories since at least the first millennium B.C., when they are recorded as having been used in China. Although the ancient Greeks and Romans used fans, they did not become widely fashionable in Europe until the fifteenth century, when Chinese and Japanese fans traveled west along the Asian trade routes and feather fans arrived from the New World. Most early fans were rigid and did not fold like those we are more familiar with today. Fans were luxury items, and it is said that they spread to France when Catherine de Medici married Henry of Orleans in 1533 and brought several with her to her new home. Feather fans from the New World inspired a fashion during the reign of Elizabeth I in England, as can be seen in the many portraits in which she is depicted carrying a fan of exotic feathers set in a handle made of precious metals and studded with gems.

By the sixteenth century, the folding fan was more common in Europe: one of the most important and earliest fans in the Museum's collection is a late sixteenth-century *découpé*, or cut-paper, fan made in France or Italy. This fan is one of only two of its type known to exist. Its sticks are made of ivory, and the leaf is created with layers of fine parchment cut to resemble a fashionable lace of the period called *reticella*.

During the seventeenth and eighteenth centuries, fans gained in popularity and artists painted them with mythological, pastoral, and courtly scenes. By the end of the eighteenth century, people in every social

***Découpé* folding fan**
Italy or France
About 1590–1600
Carved ivory sticks and cut skin leaf
with silk plain weave and mica inserts
Length of guard: 30 cm (11¾ in.)
Esther Oldham Collection 1976.182

class used fans, and new advances in printing technology made them cheaper to produce and more widely available. The subject matter ranged broadly and included souvenir fans, fans commemorating the French Revolution, and fans that served as learning tools or party favors. One of the more interesting subgenres depicts the history of ballooning, and one of the most spectacular ballooning fans was made of translucent horn painted with portraits of ballooning pioneers such as the Frenchmen Etienne Montgolfier and Jean Pierre Blanchard. Etienne Montgolfier and his brother perfected the hydrogen, or hot-air, balloon and successfully set sail from Versailles for the first time in 1773, and Blanchard, along with the American physician John Jeffries, made the first channel crossing in 1785.

Fans continued to be used during the nineteenth century and enjoyed increasing popularity under Empress Eugénie of France, who collected eighteenth-century examples. The production of fans even spread to Braintree, Massachusetts, where Edmund Sopher Hunt specialized in making folding fans. Hunt was a man of wide-ranging interests that included manufacturing fireworks, raising pears, and racing horses. The idea of mechanizing fan production intrigued him, and he received numerous patents for his work. Once he established the business successfully, he lost interest and it passed to his brother, Fred Hunt, and Frank Blake Allen, becoming the Allen Company. One of the most stunning folding fans the Allen Company produced is shaped like a luna moth and was painted by George Keiswetter, the most famous artist employed by Allen.

The majority of the fans in the Museum's collection were donated by Esther Oldham, who collected more than one thousand fans from around the world. She owned woven palm fans from the South Sea Islands, feather fans from Native America, India, and South America, and fine examples from throughout Asia. Among these is a Korean water fan (p. 114). This rigid fan is made of painted and varnished paper on a lacquered stick. It could be dipped in water and, when plied, created extra cooling due to evaporation. Oldham's gift to the MFA transformed the Museum's disparate collection of fans into one of the world's most cohesive and comprehensive.

PAP

Folding fan depicting scenes from the history of ballooning
France
About 1785
Reformed protein (molded horn) sticks and
skin leaf painted with gouache
Length of guard: 26.6 cm (10½ in.)
The Elizabeth Day McCormick Collection 43.2078

Folding fan in the shape of a luna moth
Produced by Allen Fan Company
Painted by George Keiswetter (American, born in Germany,
worked mid-19th century)
United States (East Braintree, Massachusetts)
About 1890
Carved and painted wood sticks and silk plain-weave leaf
painted in oil with applied metal sequins, thread, and net
Length of guard: 37 cm (14½ in.)
Esther Oldham Collection 1976.369

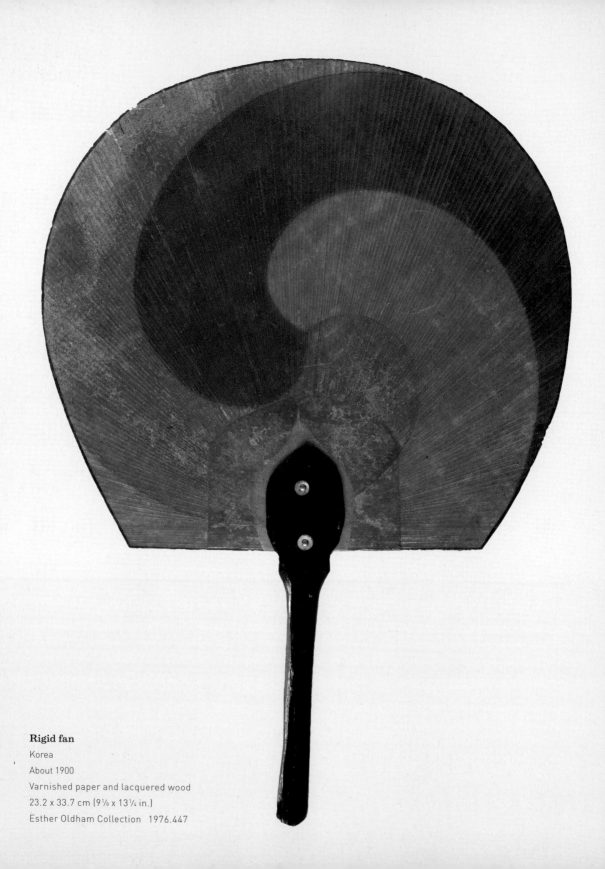

Rigid fan

Korea

About 1900

Varnished paper and lacquered wood

23.2 x 33.7 cm (9⅛ x 13¼ in.)

Esther Oldham Collection 1976.447

Costumes for the Nō Theater

Costumes made and worn for Nō, the classical drama of Japan, are among the most sophisticated and beautiful creations of the Japanese textile arts. Nō is a subtle and refined performance art combining dance, music, movement, and chant. Enacted by an all-male cast on a bare wooden stage, Nō plays tell stories of historic and legendary figures, gods, spirits, and ghosts in dreamlike and almost mystical performances full of literary and symbolic allusions. The masks and elaborate robes the actors wear serve as both costumes and moving scenery, and are essential to the overall effect and success of the performance.

Until the early seventeenth century, many Nō costumes were quite similar to the everyday clothing of the upper class, often incorporating garments donated to actors by appreciative audience members. After 1603, under the rule of the Tokugawa shoguns, Nō became a state-sponsored art form and Nō plays were performed for all important ceremonial occasions. The Tokugawa government, as part of a strategy to keep the feudal lords from acquiring too much wealth or power, encouraged them to spend lavishly on Nō costumes. By the late seventeenth century, special types of robes were being designed and made specifically for stage wear.

The main garments Nō actors wear for many roles derive from the *kosode*, a T-shaped robe with small sleeve openings worn by both men and women as everyday wear. *Atsuita* are *kosode*-like garments worn for men's roles; they take their name from the fabric originally used to make them, a stiff and heavy woven silk imported from China. Silks with woven patterns, fashionable for Imperial and upper-class military garments until the seventeenth century, continued to be used for Nō robes, and the weaving industry adapted to meet the demand for rich and effective fabrics for the stage. The silks woven for *atsuita*, in particular, have bold patterns, usually either geometric or Chinese-inspired. The early example on page 118 combines peonies and undulating lines, both motifs borrowed from China, in a simple, large-scale pattern. On stage, the robe would recall the dignity and elegance of Heian-period (794–1185) court costumes and would give an impression of decisiveness and strength.

Karaori are the main garments of female characters, but they may also be worn by some supernatural beings and as underrobes by aristocratic young warriors. How a *karaori* is draped and fastened depends on the kind of character portrayed, as does the choice of color and pattern—*karaori* with red grounds and

floral designs, for example, are considered most appropriate for young women's roles. The pattern on the robe on page 119, as on many *karaori* and *atsuita*, is organized around alternating blocks of color achieved by resist-dying the warp threads before weaving the cloth. The motifs layered over these blocks—representing the sails of ships on a sea of stylized waves, and pine trees in mist—draw the viewer into an imaginary landscape and make the robe appropriate for plays and characters associated with beaches or the sea. Achieving the correct alignment, alternation, and mirror image of the design required careful planning and meticulous weaving and construction.

Kosode made of lightweight silk plain weave or satin, decorated with embroidery and stenciled gold or silver leaf, were fashionable in the late sixteenth and early seventeenth centuries. This style has been preserved in Nō costume as the *nuihaku*. *Nuihaku* are worn for the same kinds of roles as *karaori*, but the softly draping fabric and gold-leafed surfaces make them particularly effective as underrobes or when worn in a style called *koshimaki* (waist wrap), folded down and tied over another robe as a kind of overskirt. Many early *nuihaku*, like the one illustrated on page 120, are completely covered with pattern. In this case,

the ground pattern represents bamboo strips in a basket-weave design. By edging each gold-leafed strip in brown silk embroidery, the robe's designer made them appear to pass over and under each other, creating an illusion of depth against which the lush and colorful embroidered camellia branches appear to float.

Many of the Nō robes worn as outer garments derive from Heian-period court and military robes with large open sleeves, known as *osode*. The *choken*, a loose, unlined outer robe, is usually worn by actors portraying women and female ghosts, when performing dances to instrumental music. Elegant courtier-warrior characters may also wear this style, folded and draped to imitate armor. *Choken* are usually made from transparent silk gauze brocaded with wefts of gilt paper, with the side seams left open so that the sleeves and front and back panels can float freely with the actor's movements. The robe on page 121 is unusual in having a single, unified design of weeping cherry branches across its whole width, giving it a particularly elegant and painterly quality. Cherry blossoms symbolize the beauty and promise of spring, but falling blossoms are also a metaphor for the transience of life and youth, so this robe could be worn to evoke a variety of moods.

SW

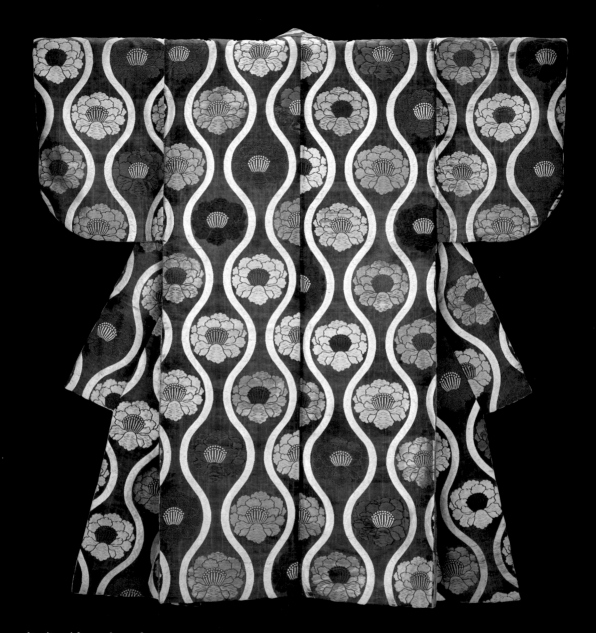

**Atsuita with peonies and
undulating lines**

Japan
Edo period, late 17th to early 18th century
Silk twill with supplementary silk
and gilt-paper patterning wefts
143.5 x 139.7 cm (56½ x 55 in.)
William Sturgis Bigelow Collection
and James Fund   15.1155

Nuihaku with bamboo lattice and
camellias

Japan

Edo period, late 17th to early 18th century

Silk satin, embroidered with silk, with
applied gold leaf

145.4 x 132.1 cm (57¼ x 52 in.)

William Sturgis Bigelow Collection

11.3792

Choken with weeping cherry branches

Japan

Edo period, 18th century

Silk gauze with supplementary gilt-paper
patterning wefts

111.8 x 214 cm (44 x 84¼ in.)

William Sturgis Bigelow Collection

11.3889

American Quilts

The first quilts acquired by colonial American house-holds during the late seventeenth and early eighteenth centuries were "whole-cloth" quilts imported mainly from England, where quilters professionally produced these bed coverings for local and export markets. Made from a single fabric—either woven silk or calamanco, a shiny wool—whole-cloth quilts were usually monochromatic with floral, scroll, or feather patterns quilted across the surface. They were prized luxury items in the Colonies, serving as symbols of conspicuous wealth in a newly emerging society.

A small crib quilt (p. 125), which possibly belonged to Mary Cooper of Boston, is an excellent example of English-made whole-cloth quilts produced in the 1740s and imported into the New England colonies. It is made of yellow silk satin, lined with silk lutestring, and stuffed with wool fleece. The quilter hand stitched across the top a pattern featuring a central medallion flanked by four quarter medallions in the corners and a lozenge outer border. This geometrical composition was inspired by the designs on Indian bedcovers and shawls, which East India trading companies imported in increasing numbers in the early eighteenth century.

The distinctly American type of cotton patchwork quilting, based on the repetition of pieced blocks of fabric, emerged in the early nineteenth century and was directly linked to developments in the textile trades. Prior to the Industrial Revolution, woven fabric was expensive and dressmakers generally used complete widths, cutting as little as possible. In-creased industrialization of the spinning, weaving, and printing of cotton, however, provided an abundance of cheap, colorful printed fabrics. Printed cotton quickly prevailed as the most popular fabric for quilts. Women in the middle and even lower classes could afford colorful calicos for their dresses, which they could then reuse as scraps for piecing. They could even purchase the prints directly to cut up and make into quilts.

Despite the popularity of printed cotton fabrics, quilters continued to make all-wool quilts in the early nineteenth century. The Paul family quilt (p. 126) is one of the rare surviving examples of this type. Made from 1830 to 1835, it was found in a trunk belonging to a descendant of William and Catherine Rice Paul, who moved to South Solon, Maine, from Greenwich, Mass-achusetts, in 1812. The actual maker is unknown, but the quilt reveals a superb design sense and excellent workmanship. The pattern features interlocking eight-pointed medallions of alternating brown and green homespun wool bordered with strips of orange wool, and an outermost edge of scalloped black wool. Within each medallion on the quilt top, the artist embroidered images, some in thick tufted yarns—pro-file portraits, believed to be of family members, and animals, such as cats, birds in trees, a leopard, and what appears to be a llama. The outermost medallions contain curious figures on horseback holding flags. A tour de force of design and execution, this quilt is a masterpiece of wool quilting.

Experimentation with block piecing yielded an abundance of new patterns by the mid-nineteenth century. Developing alongside, yet independently from, mainstream Anglo-European quilting, African American quilts tended to emphasize improvisation, bold designs, and a freeform approach to composition. One rare pictorial quilt from the late nineteenth century (p. 127) demonstrates the highly imaginative and unique vision of its maker, Harriet Powers. Born a slave in Georgia in 1837, Powers produced two known pictorial quilts. This one, the second and larger, was commissioned by a group of women, the wives of Atlanta University professors, between 1895 and 1898. It contains fifteen highly original scenes worked in a bold, freeform appliqué technique. Ten of the squares relate stories from the Bible—featuring Noah, Moses, Jonah, and Job—while the others depict extraordinary local legends and astronomical occurrences.

Powers, who could neither read nor write, most likely drew upon familiar sermons and oral folk tradition to relate these biblical and secular tales. She dictated descriptions of the individual quilt squares to Jennie Smith, a local white woman who purchased the first of Powers's quilts. Smith's transcription (now housed in the MFA's Department of Textiles and Fashion Arts) reveals Powers's subjects, which included the story of an independent hog named Betts who ran five hundred miles from Georgia to Virginia and the tale of a man frozen at his jug of liquor. The appliqué technique Powers used to create her extraordinary quilt reached its zenith in popularity in the mid to late nineteenth century. Scholars, however, have pointed out the close affinity of Powers's composition with traditional appliqué cloths from Dahomey in West Africa and Angola and the Congo in Central Africa, suggesting the survival of African cultural traditions despite slavery in America.

After the long dominance of cotton quilts, silk quilts returned to favor in the late nineteenth century with the sweeping fad for "crazy" quilts. So named for the irregular, random shapes and sizes of the silk fabric pieces, crazy quilts were most popular in the 1880s and 1890s. A unique interpretation of the crazy quilt can be seen in Celestine Bacheller's work (p. 128). Bacheller was born in Lynn, Massachusetts, in 1839 and lived in the Wyoma neighborhood, known for its silk dye houses. Her father, Alfred, was a silk dyer, so the silks used in the quilt may have been remnants from his trade. Bacheller's quilt features twelve vignettes pieced and embroidered from lush, colorful silk satins and velvets. She altered the standard format, however, by creating unusual and complex architectural and landscape scenes. Bacheller transformed three-story houses with gardens, rocky coastlines, and sailboats—real sites found around her home in Lynn—into ornate, dense patchwork squares in her quilt.

LDW

Crib quilt
England (made for American market)
About 1744
Silk satin, backed with silk plain weave
and quilted
122.3 x 98.5 cm (48⅛ x 38¾ in.)
Gift of Miss Katherine Amory Homans
45.779

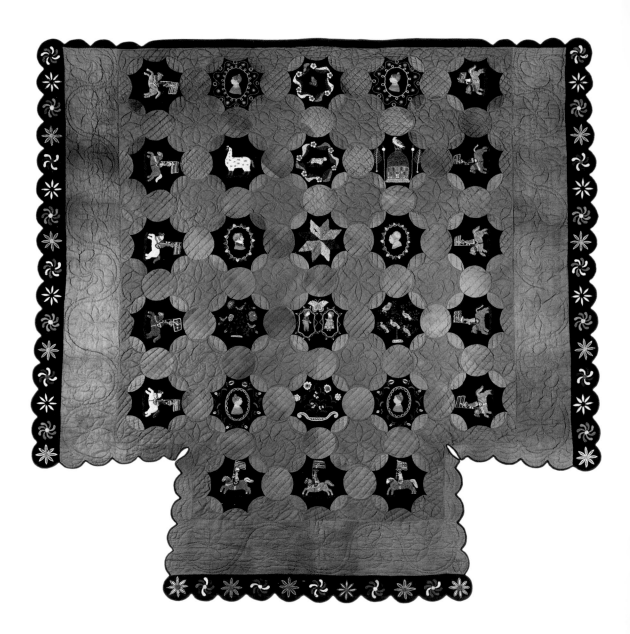

Quilt

United States (South Solon, Maine)

1830–35

Wool plain weave, pieced, embroidered, and quilted

266.7 x 269.2 cm (105 x 106 in.)

Museum purchase with funds donated from
the Marshall H. Gould Fund, Joyce and Edward Linde,
and an anonymous supporter   2005.95

Pictorial quilt

Harriet Powers (1837–1911)

United States (Athens, Georgia)

1895–98

Cotton plain weave, pieced, appliquéd,

embroidered, and quilted

175 x 266.7 cm (68⅞ x 105 in.)

Bequest of Maxim Karolik 64.619

Quilt

Celestine Bacheller (1839–about 1922)

United States

(Wyoma, Lynn, Massachusetts)

1875–1900

Silk plain weave, velvet, and satin, pieced
and embroidered

188.8 x 144.6 cm (74¼ x 57 in.)

Gift of Mr. and Mrs. Edward J. Healy in
memory of Mrs. Charles O'Malley   63.655

European Printed Textiles

The development of the European printed-textile industry was directly linked to several factors: the trade in printed cottons from India, technological innovations, and shifting popular tastes. Up until the sixteenth century, European printed-textile manufacturing was a secondary industry that produced block-printed fabrics largely in imitation of the costly woven silks and wools favored in contemporary dress. The arrival of exotic printed cottons from India, however, sparked an enduring taste for bright, lightweight, and colorfast cottons that challenged the dominance of the silk- and wool-weaving industries and stimulated the expansion of a domestic printed-textile industry to compete with these new imports.

Indian hand-painted and block-printed cottons in the form of bedcovers, called *palampores*, and dress goods first arrived in Europe in the sixteenth century via the various East India trading companies. Soon Europeans were infatuated with the exotic floral patterns and the durability of their colors. The block-printed cottons could withstand repeated washings without fading, owing to the Indian textile printers' mastery of mordants (natural metallic or mineral agents used to fix dyes), a printing technique hitherto unknown in Europe.

As the demand for Indian imports increased to an obsession in the seventeenth century, and as prices spiked, European textile printers sought to gain a share of the lucrative market by printing cottons that duplicated not only the exotic floral patterns of Indian imports but also the mordant technology behind them. The close connection between European and Indian printed cottons can be seen in this dress dated to 1785. Printed in France, the polonaise robe with matching quilted petticoat reveals a faithful imitation of the curling, exotic floral designs of an earlier Indian printed cotton. The French version also demonstrates the successful mastery of the Indian mordant method; it was block-printed with alum and iron mordants prior to dyeing with traditional European dyestuffs such as madder (for red) and weld (for yellow).

The popularity of Indian cottons generated violent opposition from European wool and silk weavers. Under pressure from these groups, the French government issued the first of several strict decrees in 1686 banning the wearing and manufacture of "toiles de cotton peinte des Indes," thereby strangling both the fledgling domestic industry and the imported textile market, until 1759 when the ban was repealed. The English government followed suit with its own ban on the importation, use, and wearing of Indian "calicoes" in 1701. Ironically, this restriction only served to assist the nascent English textile-printing industry, as domestically printed textiles were still legal. Although further legislation enacted in 1720 limited domestic production to printing on Irish linen or fustian, a cotton and linen mix, English manufacturers continued to expand production of printed cottons for large export markets in Africa, Asia, and the Americas, until the ban was fully repealed in 1774.

In the mid-eighteenth century, the recently invented process of copperplate printing opened a new chapter in European textile printing. Employing an incised sheet of copper (thirty-six inches square), copperplate printing was closely related to intaglio printing with engraved metal plates on paper. The new technique allowed much larger repeats as well as significantly finer linear effects and shading than could be achieved with wood blocks. However, the larger repeat made printing multiple colors with additional plates difficult, so copperplate prints were limited to a single color—red, blue, purple, or sepia—with additional colors added by wood blocks or hand painting. Nevertheless, the new copperplate technique enabled more accurate reproduction of images and stimulated a taste for pictorial subjects of figures derived from engraved prints.

fig. 17 (above) **Indian hand-painted and printed cottons such as this one provided inspiration for European textile makers.**

Dress and petticoat
France
About 1785, altered at a later date
Cotton plain weave, block-printed
Center back length: overdress 147 cm (58 in.),
petticoat 89 cm (35 in.)
The Elizabeth Day McCormick Collection 43.1619

One of the earliest dated examples of a design from a copperplate is this English printed cotton inscribed "R. Iones 1761." It was printed for export by Robert Jones, one of several successful textile printers operating in England in the mid-eighteenth century, at his manufactory at Old Ford in the East End of London. (An *I* was often used in place of a *J* in seventeenth- and eighteenth-century print typography.) The cotton features a bucolic scene of figures and animals set among classical ruins that was taken from an etching executed in 1652 by the Flemish artist Nicholas Berghem.

In 1759 France finally lifted the ban on printed cottons, opening the door to a number of new print manufactories. German-born Christophe-Philippe Oberkampf established one of the most important, a factory in Jouy-en-Josas outside of Paris. The printworks of Oberkampf produced some of the finest printed cottons in the late eighteenth and early nineteenth centuries and was particularly noted for its figurative copperplate-engraved textiles.

Jean-Baptiste Huet, a leading French artist of the period, designed the fabric *Les Losanges*, printed at Oberkampf about 1800. Its flat, geometric, compartmentalized design featuring medallions is typical of furnishing fabrics from that time and reflects the prevailing taste for Neoclassicism in art. The design celebrates the classical Greek emblems of the harvest. One of the oval medallions contains an altar to Demeter, goddess of agriculture, attended by priestesses making a sacrifice. This and the other images in the medallions and grid derive from engravings of antiquities in popular eighteenth-century books.

In 1783 the Scotsman Thomas Bell patented a mechanized method for printing with engraved rollers. This new technology allowed much faster printing of cotton, and English manufacturers had adopted it full-scale by 1815. The nature of the cylinders with their continuous rolling edge, however, made the printing of small repeat patterns—florals or geometrics—most effective. In the second decade of the nineteenth century, roller-printed patterns would become increasingly abundant but also cheaper in quality.

LDW

Les Losanges furnishing fabric
Designed by Jean-Baptiste Huet (1745–1811)
Printed by Oberkampf Manufactory
France (Jouy-en-Josas)
About 1800
Cotton plain weave, copperplate-printed
90.7 x 95.8 cm (35¾ x 37¾ in.)
Gift of Mrs. Edward C. Streeter   59.1042

Length of furnishing fabric (left)
Printed by Robert Jones (English, worked second half of
18th century) after a design by Nicholas Berghem (Dutch,
1620–1683)
England (Old Ford, London)
1761
Cotton plain weave, copperplate-printed
199.5 x 89 cm (78½ x 35 in.)
Transfer from Decorative Arts   60.177

Ball dress
United States or France
About 1858
Silk plain weave (taffeta), machine net (tulle),
and silk bobbin lace, trimmed with silk ribbon,
embroidered silk net, and silk flowers
Center back length: bodice 34.9 cm (13¾ in.),
skirt 111.8 cm (44 in.)
Gift of Ronald T. Lyman 51.1346a–b

Early to Mid-Nineteenth-Century Fashion

Tremendous social, political, and economic changes occurred during the first half of the nineteenth century. Increased mechanization (the result of the Industrial Revolution), greater prosperity, a growing middle class, and shifting cultural values all affected the constantly evolving fashions of the period. Women's garments revealed the greatest transformation, moving from a relaxed, natural shape inspired by classical ideals to an increasingly structured and tailored silhouette.

The century opened with a style of women's dress consciously evocative of classical models. Characterized by a low neckline, high waistline, and narrow skirts falling in natural folds, this style had become popular at the end of the eighteenth century in a society that embraced changing political ideas strongly influenced by Enlightenment notions of naturalism and freedom. The preferred fabrics were sheer white muslins. Gathered under the bust with side or front ties, the resulting columnar gown emulated the graceful drapery seen on ancient sculpture and vases greatly admired in this period.

The fashionable gown on page 136 is a striking example of the prevailing classical taste in dress. Made between 1800 and 1805, the apex of Grecian-style dress, the formal gown features short sleeves, an extremely high waistline, and a narrow, tubular skirt falling into an extended train behind. Its maker hand embroidered the white cotton gauze fabric with brilliant red wool and white cotton thread in an allover pattern of floral sprigs, with wide bands of scrolling Greek key pattern and laurel branches. The cut of the dress, its costly imported Indian fabric, and the quality of its embroidery suggest a French origin.

Other inspirations began to affect fashion in the second decade of the nineteenth century, as the simplicity and restraint of classically inspired dress yielded to the artifice, ornamentation, and extravagance of the Romantic period. Nostalgia for historical eras (other than ancient Greece and Rome) was reflected in full skirts, ruffs and "vandyked" lace collars and cuffs, and fanciful slashed and puffed sleeves and hems, all popularly referred to as "gothic" details.

By the mid-1820s, a pronounced hourglass silhouette—distinguished by expanding skirts, a small waist located in a natural position, and full sleeves, which inflated to enormous proportions by the end of the decade—had emerged as the fashionable look. It was achieved through increasingly complex tailoring and structured undergarments, including tightly laced, whale-boned corsets and layers of petticoats. To balance the widening skirts, enormous and elaborate coiffures and hats became fashionable. The range of fabrics increased, with silks and cottons roller-printed in colorful patterns becoming increasingly popular.

A ball gown made between 1825 and 1830 reveals the fanciful extravagance of formal dress during this period (p. 137). The cream silk-satin gown features a low, round neckline, enormous puffed sleeves, and a full skirt gathered into the waistline. Gilt metal embroidery, worked into textured and flat gold wire,

embellishes it in an allover pattern of floral sprigs, with a deep border pattern of wheat sheaves and three-dimensional floral branches.

The fashions that appeared in the 1850s resulted from a confluence of style and technology. Increased use of sewing machines (first patented in the 1840s) began to affect the production of clothing, as machine stitching replaced hand sewing. The expanded use of mechanized lace machines (Heathcote's bobbin net machine was patented in 1808) and the automated jacquard loom revolutionized the textile industries. The most notorious invention of the 1850s was the steel hoop skirt, introduced in 1856. This affordable device, made of concentric steel hoops sewn to cotton tapes, enabled skirts to reach enormous widths. While technology made fashion more affordable and accessible to the middle and lower classes, an increasingly complex etiquette surrounding the correct type of garments for specific occasions evolved and preserved elite social status.

Formal dress
France
1800–1805
Cotton gauze, embroidered with
wool and cotton
Center back length: 235 cm (91½ in.)
Gift of Miss Eleanora Curtis   22.665

The womanly ideal in the 1850s featured floor-length, bell-shaped skirts, a small waist (achieved through tight steel-boned corsets), and gently sloping shoulders, either revealed in evening dress or covered during daytime with sleeves that flared at the wrist. Particularly stylish mid-1850s skirts required ever-increasing amounts of specialized fabrics, in patterns woven to shape. Evening dress was distinguished from day dress by short sleeves and very low neck-lines. The most formal events, such as balls, demanded the most luxurious fabric.

The dress on page 134, a confection in pink silk, epitomizes the exuberance of mid-nineteenth-century ball gowns. Its five tiers of machine-made silk tulle are trimmed with brocaded ribbons and fitted over a silk taffeta skirt and bodice. With prodigious yardage, opulent trimmings (both hand- and machine-made laces and woven ribbons), and elaborate accessories, women's dresses such as this functioned as the outward manifestations of prosperity, ingenuity, and innovation.

LDW

Ball dress

France

1825–30

Silk satin, embroidered with metallic threads

Center back length: 121.5 cm (47¹³/₁₆ in.)

The Elizabeth Day McCormick Collection 43.1650

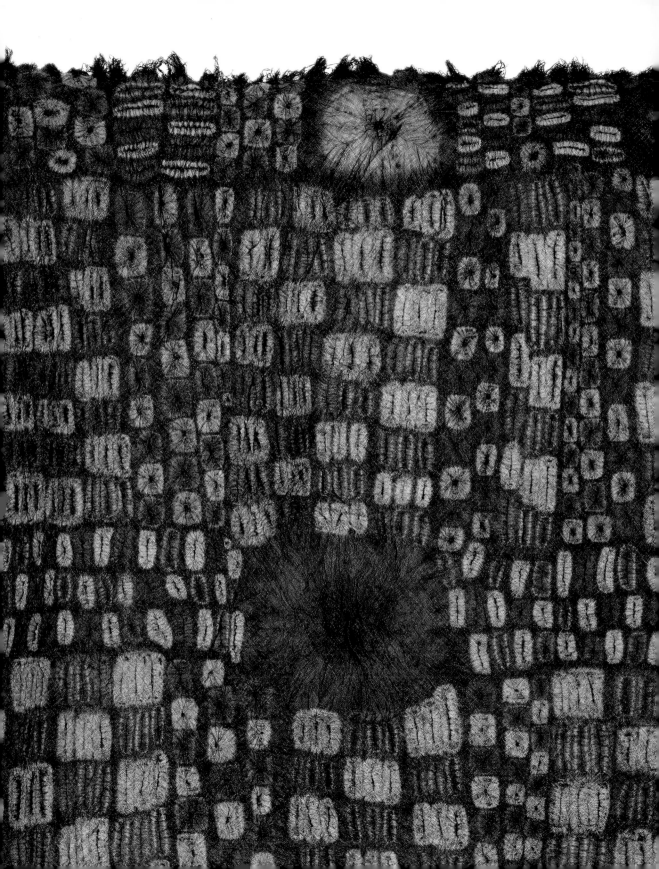

Textiles from Sub-Saharan Africa

A rich textile tradition exists in sub-Saharan Africa, whose inhabitants traditionally exploited native materials such as bark and palm-leaf fiber, or raffia, to create clothing for daily and ceremonial use. As foreign trade introduced new materials and techniques, Africans adopted and adapted these to suit their lifestyle. Developing commerce with North Africa brought cotton and wool to the sub-Saharan region by the tenth century, and contact with the West after the end of the fifteenth century brought silk, wool cloth, and printed textiles. Today, Africans have adapted to the global economy and use rayon, polyester, lurex, and other synthetic fibers. Textile-printing factories have opened throughout West Africa.

While most sub-Saharan Africans adapted their textile traditions to new materials and techniques, some of the oldest African traditions, such as the use of bark cloth and raffia, survived well into the nineteenth century. The use of these materials continued in parts of the continent that had been inaccessible or of no trade interest to the Arabs from the north or Europeans from the west. This included most of the inland areas around the Congo River, where the Mangbetu, Mbuti, and Pygmy peoples continued to produce bark loincloths and aprons into the nineteenth century.

A Mangbetu chief's loincloth (p. 140), or *nogi*, collected early in the twentieth century by Belgian Dominican friars is an example of such a surviving clothing tradition. The Mangbetu people traveled to the Congo region from Sudan in the nineteenth century and intermixed with the Pygmy and Mbuti people already living there. Mangbetu men and women, like the Pygmy and the Mbuti, wore loincloths made out of bark. Men's cloths were bigger than women's and were worn pleated, wrapped around the lower body and held in place with a belt. The bark comes from various species of fig trees, the most common being the *Ficus natalensis*. The Mangbetu people planted these trees conveniently near family homes and, when needed, cut the bark from the trees and pounded it to create a soft, malleable cloth. In order to make the loincloth big enough, they stitched together smaller pieces of bark cloth. The combination of dark brown and natural bark in this loincloth resulted in a dramatic, minimal composition.

Another indigenous material used by sub-Saharan Africans was raffia palm fiber. To create this material, they pulled apart palm leaves and drew out fiber strands 90 to 150 centimeters (35 to 59 inches) long. Then they dried the fibers and wove or plaited them into fine cloth. Several peoples continued the tradition of weaving with raffia into the nineteenth century, including the Dida of Ivory Coast and the Kuba of the Congo. Clothing made of raffia was an important status symbol for both the Dida and the Kuba. The Dida people plaited raffia fibers to create loincloths for women and large mantles for men. They made these wrappers without a loom, manipulating each thread by hand to create a plain-weave structure; the scale of the finished textiles implies highly skilled labor. They

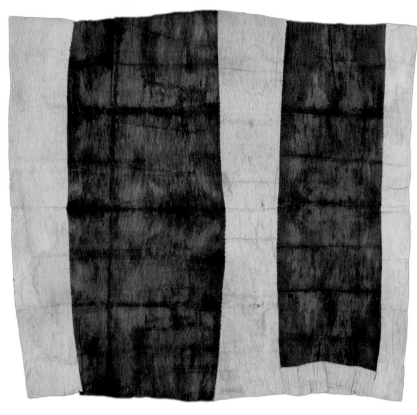

Chief's loincloth (*nogi*)
Mangbetu people
Republic of the Congo
First half of the 20th century
Bark cloth, mud-dyed and stitched with raffia
112.4 x 117.5 cm (44¼ x 46¼ in.)
Museum purchase with funds donated by Jeremy and Hanne Grantham   2004.2055

then tie-dyed the garments, giving them a highly textured surface. The man's wrapper at right, probably made about 1900, illustrates the sophisticated designs the Dida achieved through tie-dyeing.

The Kuba wore elaborately embroidered raffia skirts for ceremonial purposes. High-status women wore skirts called *ntchak* that wrapped around the waist and were characterized by a border made of bundled reeds that produced a wavy outer edge. The *ntchak* illustrated on page 142 was produced using traditional materials and takes the traditional form. However, the main field of the skirt, created by weaving the raffia fibers on a loom, is decorated with pulled and drawn work, European embroidery techniques that the maker may have learned from Belgian missionaries who proselytized in the Congo.

One of the earliest and most influential materials introduced into sub-Saharan Africa was cotton. Cotton reached West Africa across the Saharan trade routes and became an important crop by the eleventh century. West Africans adopted not only the new material but also the looms used by the nomads of the Sahara. They wove narrow strips, often more than 60 meters (200 feet) long, and then cut them and stitched them together to make wrappers for men and women. While this tradition exists throughout West Africa, it is the cloth of the Ashante of Ghana, known as *kente*, that has become most famous. The Ewe, who also live in Ghana, produced beautiful, inventive cloth in a manner similar to the Ashante. The Ewe wrapper pictured on page 143 is rare both in its design and in the technique in which it is woven. Large blocks of pattern and color enliven the cloth, in contrast to the smaller, more densely packed designs of traditional Ewe and Ashante *kente*. The weaver used a second warp that changes the color on one face of the cloth, giving it two unique sides.

PAP

Man's wrapper

Dida people

Ivory Coast

About 1900

Raffia, plaited and tie-dyed

151 x 151 cm (59 ½ x 59 ½ in.)

Frederick Brown Fund, Textile Income Pur-
chase Fund, The Elizabeth Day McCormick
Collection by exchange, and Alice J. Morse
Fund   2000.575

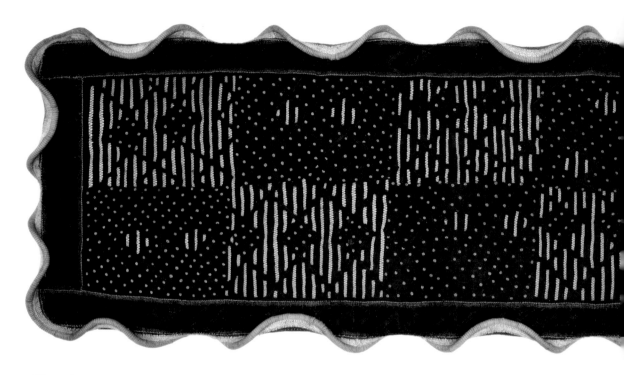

Woman's ceremonial skirt (*ntchak*)
Bushong people
Republic of the Congo (Kuba kingdom)
First half of the 20th century
Raffia plain weave, embroidered with pulled
and drawn work
68.7 x 151 cm (27 x 59½ in.)
Benjamin and Lucy Rowland Fund   1995.91

Man's wrapper
Ewe people
Ghana
20th century
Cotton plain weave with supplementary
patterning warps and wefts
284.5 x 165 cm (112 x 65 in.)
Museum purchase with funds donated by
Jeremy and Hanne Grantham   2004.676

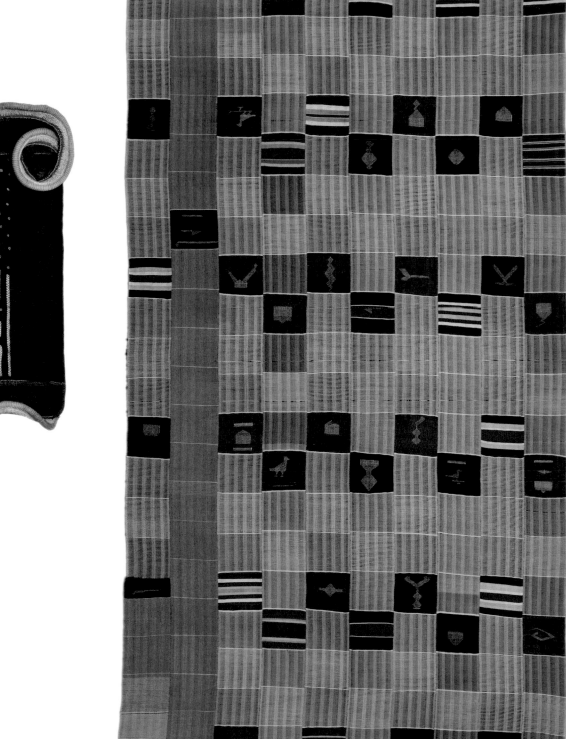

Greek Islands Embroideries

Domestic embroideries made in the Greek islands and the mainland coastal region of Epirus vividly reflect the influx of diverse artistic influences into this region and tell of its long, and often turbulent, history as a crossroads for trade between east and west. Over time, various foreign powers, including the Byzantine Empire, the Frankish-Venetian empire, and the Ottoman Turks, have occupied each of the island groups located in the Ionian and Aegean seas—the Ionian Islands, the Sporades, the Northern Islands, the Cyclades, the Dodecanese, and Crete. Each group possesses a distinctive style of embroidery, whose patterns and motifs have been passed down from generation to generation and, through travel and marriage, from one island to another. In the nineteenth century, however, political revolution, social change, and industrialization all but extinguished this traditional handicraft.

Although professional embroiderers existed, young women historically worked most of the embroideries for their dowries. A dowry usually consisted of an embroidered wedding costume along with woven and embroidered home furnishings such as bedcovers and hangings that were used for the wedding night and other festive occasions. These highly prized possessions served as an expression of cultural heritage, as well as family wealth and prestige. Embroidered furnishings also brought a distinct and cohesive aesthetic to the simple one-room homes that many islanders occupied, while serving a utilitarian pur-pose such as dividing a room into public and private spaces.

The figural composition on the cushion cover pictured on page 146 is characteristic of a group of embroideries attributed to Epirus. Textile historians often categorize embroideries from Epirus with those from the nearby Ionian Islands, because they share more in common with island work than with other mainland embroideries. Yanina, the capital of Epirus, was the seat of the famous eighteenth-century Turkish ruler Ali Pasha, whose lavish court made Epirus a textile center and trade hub. The stylized hyacinths and tulips, along with the men's costumes, display a strong Turkish influence. Extant cushion covers from this area commonly depict bridal parties or, as in this example, horsemen surrounded by simplified floral motifs and animals. Historically, this cover has also been attributed to the Ionian Islands, which at the time were controlled by the Venetians; island residents may have had contact with the mainland through trade and travel, bringing the Ottoman-inspired motifs into their work.

Also displaying an Ottoman influence is an eighteenth-century bedcover (p. 147) from Skyros, the largest island in the Northern Sporades. Embroideries from this area are characterized by a variety of whimsical, freely drawn motifs ranging from flowers, animals, and ships to fantastical creatures such as harpies and sphinxes that have their origins in the arts of ancient Egypt and Persia. This bedcover, comprised

of three lengths joined with yellow and blue striped ribbon, depicts fantastical peacock-like birds and a tree-of-life motif. The middle panel, which was probably a nineteenth-century addition by a daughter or granddaughter, shows a central medallion flanked on either side by birds and flowers and men smoking pipes.

For the people of the Dodecanese, the wedding bed tent was perhaps the most sacred, and certainly the most elaborately decorated, of domestic textiles. The tradition of the nuptial bed tent is distinctive to these islands and results from the structure of their beds, which were built on raised, corner platforms and required more privacy than a curtain could offer. The front of a bed tent, like the example from Kos seen on page 148, was usually the most decorated part. Worked primarily in cross-stitch, this pattern consists of stylized floral and geometric designs similar to those found in Mamluk Egyptian embroidery. More figural compositions, such as the parrots, double-headed eagle, and sailing ships on this example, usually appear at the top of a tent's opening.

The friezelike composition illustrated on the face of a cushion cover (p. 149) from Crete strongly shows the European, particular Venetian, influence on island embroideries. Surviving costumes and home furnishings from this area display either a monochromatic palette of red or blue, like this example, or a brilliant polychromatic palette. The double-tailed mermaid, birds, insects, double-headed eagle, and scrolling flowers, all worked in a rich blue satin stitch, are similar to those found in Italian silks and laces. Venetian pattern books, which also incorporated motifs that originated in Byzantine and Near Eastern art, made their way to the islands in the sixteenth century.

TWH

Cushion cover (above)
Greece (Epirus or Ionian Islands)
18th or 19th century
Linen plain weave, embroidered with silk
53.5 x 43 cm (21 1/16 x 16 15/16 in.)
The Elizabeth Day McCormick
Collection 43.374

Bedcover (right)
Greece (Skyros, Northern Sporades)
18th or 19th century
Linen plain weave, embroidered with silk
161 x 245 cm (63 3/8 x 96 7/16 in.)
Gift in the name of Abby L. Tyler 33.23

Panels from a bed tent

Greece (Kos, Dodecanese)

18th or 19th century

Linen plain weave, embroidered

with silk

329.1 x 256.7 cm (129½ x 101 in.)

Gift of Mrs. Solomon R. Guggenheim 50.2625

One face of a cushion cover

Greece (Crete)

18th or 19th century

Linen and cotton plain weave,

embroidered with silk

49.5 x 38.1 cm (19½ x 15 in.)

Collection of Mr. and Mrs. Harry A. Hill 1971.437

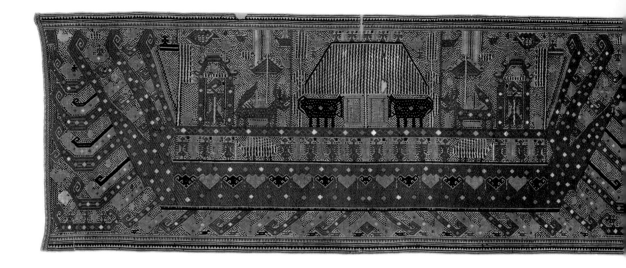

Sumatran Textiles

Sumatra is the western-most island of the seventeen thousand islands that make up the republic of Indonesia. Its location made it an important stop along the sea trade routes between East Asia and India by the tenth century and with Europe by the sixteenth century. The island's importance in the spice trade—pepper was one of its most lucrative export commodities —and its rich natural resources brought the people living in the coastal trading towns of the north great wealth and introduced them to a rich array of foreign influences from India, China, and the West. The Minangkabau people of West Sumatra were avid traders and developed a rich textile tradition that incorporated gold- and silver-wrapped yarns. In southern Sumatra, the people of Lampong became wealthy due to the pepper trade but did not have such close contact with foreigners, because the northern Javanese handled the pepper trade in the region. Lampong textiles thus show less foreign influence but are an equally rich tradition.

One of the most distinctive types of textiles woven in Lampong was hung during important ceremonies related to birth, naming, marriage, and death. The hangings are known as "ship cloths" because many are patterned with large ships laden with people and ani-

mals. The ship was a common image for the seafaring Indonesians and probably symbolized a state of transition, thus making it appropriate for ceremonies related to significant life events. A multi-tiered ship, as seen here, also represented the social order: only rulers within specific governing groups known as *marga* could use this symbol. Red ships denoted the sacred realm, whereas blue ships identified the earthly realm.

Another characteristic cloth the Lampong people produced was a woman's ceremonial sarong called a *tapis*. Ceremonies and accompanying feasts played an important role in Lampong culture and served as displays of wealth and of an individual's rise through the social order. Elaborately patterned ceremonial dress included *tapis* that were patterned with horizontal bands of ikat alternating with strips of embroidery. The designs show little influence from foreign sources and, like the "ship cloth," may represent a long-standing Lampong tradition. Researchers have often referred to the amoeba-like sea creatures that inhabit the embroidered bands in the cloth pictured on page 152 as squids or octopi, but their actual meaning is now lost. Women who lived in the mountainous regions in southern Sumatra wore this style of *tapis*.

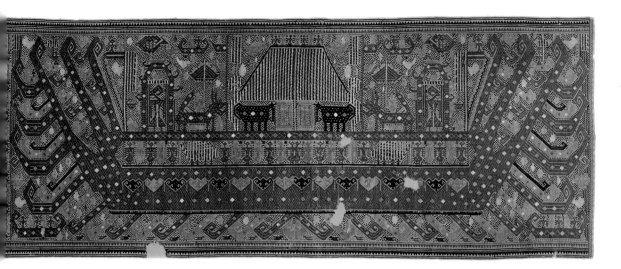

While the Lampong people of southern Sumatra appear to have maintained their traditional designs over the centuries, the people of northern Sumatra incorporated foreign design influences and material into their textiles. The Minangkabau people of West Sumatra live in a mountainous region rich in natural resources. They were successful traders and many made long journeys over the mountains to reach the eastern shore, where the major seafaring ports were located. As a result, the Minangkabau textile traditions evolved over the years, incorporating new design motifs and materials such as silk and gold- and silver-wrapped threads. The wealth of the Minangkabau also ensured the creation of lavish textiles that played an important role in ceremony and in daily life.

Minangkabau women wore elaborately folded headdresses called *kain tangkuluak*. They wrapped these headcloths to form two points, similar to the horns of the water buffalo. This shape is common in Minangkabau culture and appears in one of the most important buildings in the village, the *adat*, or belief, house owned by matrilineal lineage and used by the family for meetings, councils, and ceremonial activities; its roof is shaped with two points on either side. The connection between the house and the headdress emphasizes the important role of women in matrilineal Minangkabau culture. The headcloth shown on page 153 displays traditional designs that are laden with meaning. The motif of *kunang kunang*, or fireflies, inspires hope because of the manner in which fireflies light up the villages at night, and interlacing bands known as *ulek tantadu*, or caterpillars on parade, symbolize the fact that caterpillars who are moving together in a line are not eating the plants and flowers along the way. This is understood to mean that a good Minangkabau does not stray from tradition and behave destructively.

PAP

Ceremonial hanging (*palepai*)
Southern Sumatra (Lampong region)
Mid-19th century
Cotton plain weave with supplementary
patterning wefts
73.7 x 283 cm (29 x 150½ in.)
The William E. Nickerson Fund No. 2   1980.172

Woman's ceremonial skirt (*tapis*)

Southern Sumatra (Lampong region)

19th century

Cotton plain weave, ikat dyed

and embroidered with silk

129 x 119 cm (50 ¾ x 47 in.)

Otis Norcross Fund   1980.281

Woman's headcloth (detail)

Minangkabau people

West Sumatra (Pariangan/Batipuah region)

19th century

Silk plain weave with supplementary silk

and metal-wrapped patterning wefts

264 x 78 cm (104 x 30 ¾ in.)

Gift of Mrs. Clifford Smith   38.82

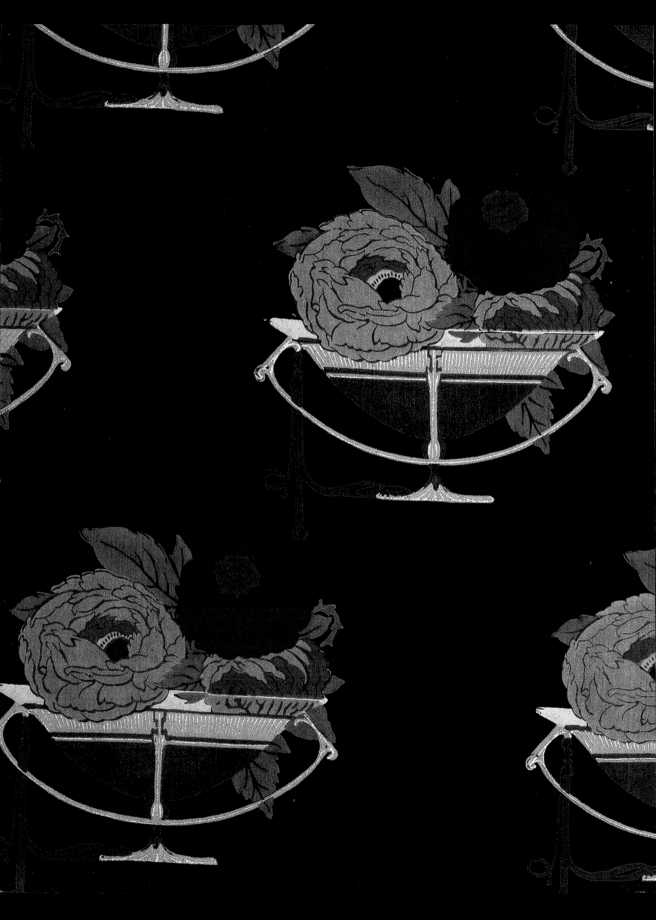

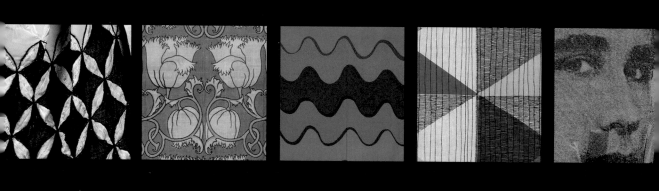

The Modern World 1875–2005

In the wake of the Industrial Revolution, artists, designers, and philosophers responded in various ways to the mechanization of textile manufacturing. Commentators such as William Morris and John Ruskin fought against the effects of mass production in the late nineteenth century in an effort to bring good design and handcraftsmanship back to the textile arts. Later, during the first decades of the twentieth century, artists and designers achieved a marriage of art and industry in the sophisticated textiles of the Art Deco style. Some forward-looking manufacturers and design schools, such as the Bauhaus in Germany, explored the potential of mechanization and emphasized good design for mass production, while artists like Marguerite Zorach and Sonia Delaunay experimented with batik, embroidery, and other craft techniques to create one-of-a-kind works of art. In the late 1950s artists such as Ed Rossbach, Lenore Tawney, and Sheila Hicks, many of whom were taught by Bauhaus-trained émigrés to the United States, reinterpreted traditional textile techniques in their work and became leaders in the emerging Fiber Art movement of the 1960s and 1970s.

Fashion also underwent dramatic changes during this period. Increased sophistication in the making of custom garments ushered in the era of haute couture, labels, and named designers. In combination with the expanded reach of fashion magazines, these developments had a profound impact on the art and industry of fashion. The model of Paris grand couture, started by Charles Frederick Worth in the nineteenth century, survived into the mid-twentieth century but was challenged by the emergence of the ready-to-wear industry. After World War II, Parisian designers such as Cristóbal Balenciaga and Madame Grès shared the stage with a new wave of young designers from Britain and the United States who advocated more casual, democratic, and accessible fashions.

fig. 18 Early twentieth-century fashion plates are characterized by simple lines and flat color that reflect the streamlined silhouette of the period.

WORTH & BOBERGH

7. RUE DE LA PAIX 7. PARI

Worth and the Birth of Couture

Charles Frederick Worth is generally recognized as the father of modern haute couture—high-end, custom dressmaking. Worth not only created some of the most elegant and coveted garments of the late nineteenth century, he also revolutionized dressmaking and established a modern approach to the business of fashion.

Worth was an unlikely champion of fashion. An Englishman, born in Lincolnshire in 1825, he came from a family of solicitors but entered the dry goods trade in the late 1830s. He apprenticed with two London silk merchants, receiving important training in textile connoisseurship and English tailoring practices. In the 1840s he moved to Paris to better his fortunes. After working at Gagelin-Opigez et Cie., the preeminent textile dealer in Paris who supplied rich Lyon silks and trims, he established a dressmaking enterprise in partnership with Otto Gustav Bobergh. Worth and Bobergh opened for trade at 7, rue de la Paix in the autumn/winter of 1857–58. By 1860 the firm had secured its first important customer, Pauline, Princess von Metternich, a vital member of the Second Empire court of France, who was followed shortly by another major client, Eugénie, Empress of France.

fig. 19 Worth's earliest dress designs bore the label "Worth and Bobergh," stamped in gold, indicating his early partnership with Otto Gustav Bobergh.

Worth ultimately dressed most of the aristocracy of Europe, as well as socially prominent Americans. His novel business practices changed not only the way designers made dresses but also the way they marketed them. Until the mid-nineteenth century, dressmakers were technicians who created garments following the client's wishes from already purchased fabric. In contrast, Worth presented his creations—fabric, cut, and construction—as a whole concept, establishing his own taste as paramount in achieving the right look. He was a perfectionist, and his gowns soon became widely known for their sumptuous fabrics and impeccable cut and finish.

Worth personally supervised designs for important clients, who flocked to his atelier, making it a destination for the fashionable elite. More importantly, he expanded the practice of selling "models" to fashion retailers in Europe and America, who copied them for local clients—a couture practice that would become standard in the twentieth century. He also further popularized the custom of labeling garments. His earliest labels bear the name "Worth and Bobergh," the partnership that lasted until 1870. After that year, the firm continued under the sole direction of Charles Frederick Worth and became known as the House of Worth.

Dresses with historical inspiration were a particular specialty of the House of Worth. A two-piece afternoon dress (p. 161) made about 1880 reveals the elegance of Worth's designs and his enduring interest in historical styles. It features a stylish, tight-fitting bodice and bustle skirt with train. Several details, however, evoke styles of a century before, including the low, square neckline, stomacher-like center bow, and three-quarter length ruffled sleeves, as well as the split skirt construction, which suggests a petticoat underneath. Even the fabric—cut velvet with a small-scale feather-and-bow pattern—is reminiscent of the delicate, pastel fashions of the Rococo taste.

Worth's extensive understanding of fabrics allowed him to incorporate textile patterns into the whole-design concept of his garments. Through connections fostered early in his career, he had unprecedented opportunities to influence patterns of silks woven at the Lyon silk mills. The reception or dinner dress on page 162, from about 1883, features a deep burgundy red silk damask patterned with tulip blossoms. Tassanari & Chatel, a silk manufacturer in Lyon who over the years provided many fabrics to the House of Worth, likely wove the stunning fabric. The tulip damask forms a deep V-pointed bodice, with three-quarter length sleeves and a square neckline trimmed with lace in a loose interpretation of fashions from the 1690s. Worth employed the fabric again in the skirt over a plain silk faille petticoat, drawing it to the rear in an elaborate bustle that cascades down into an extended train. Dense glass-bead gimp completes both the skirt and bodice fronts, adding richness and complexity to this elegant ensemble.

Fabric plays an equally integral role in the design of an evening gown dated to the early 1890s (p. 163). The striking two-piece outfit is made of pink ribbed silk patterned allover with a pea-pod lattice design.

Strings of black beads cascade asymmetrically down the front of the bodice, while black silk ribbons drape across the front and gather in a bow at the bodice back. More interesting, however, is the skirt treatment. The elaborately beaded black net trim that covers the lower front half of the skirt was carefully trimmed and stitched to reveal the pea pods below, producing a bold lattice design in reverse appliqué.

LDW

Afternoon dress
Charles Frederick Worth (English, worked in France, 1825–1895) for the House of Worth
France (Paris)
About 1880
Silk plain weave (faille), silk satin, and silk cut and uncut velvet, trimmed with silk plain weave (chiffon) and silk fringe
Center back length: bodice 59.1 cm (23¼ in), skirt 113 cm (44½ in)
Gift of Mrs. Hugh D. Scott 50.803a–b

Reception or dinner dress

Charles Frederick Worth (English, worked in
France, 1825–1895) for the House of Worth

France (Paris)

About 1883

Silk damask, satin, and plain weave (taffeta),
trimmed with glass beads and metallic yarn gimp,
with silk fringe and machine-made lace

Center back length: bodice 69.8 cm (27 ½ in.),
skirt 177.5 cm (71 in.)

Gift of Mrs. Robert Homans 46.199a–b

Evening dress

Charles Frederick Worth (English, worked in France,
1825–1895) for the House of Worth
France (Paris)
About 1893
Silk plain weave patterned with
weft floats, trimmed with silk
plain weave (chiffon), satin ribbons,
jet beads, and machine net
Center back length: bodice 35.7 cm (90¾ in.),
skirt 151 cm (59½ in.)
Gift of Mrs. Robert Homans   46.204a–b

Lo silken my garden & silken my sky, And silken the apple boughs hanging on high

The English Arts and Crafts Movement

The Arts and Crafts Movement had its origins in the mid-nineteenth century, when a number of British architects, artists, and critics began to react against what they saw as the dehumanizing effects of the Industrial Revolution and the soullessness and ugliness of modern architecture and manufactured goods. Looking to the preindustrial past, in particular the Middle Ages, they called for a return to simplicity and honesty in materials and construction, advised artists to find inspiration in direct observation of nature, and advocated that art should be an integral part of daily life. Above all, the leaders of the movement called for the revival of traditional handcrafts, which they believed would have a positive effect on both art and society.

Among the most important figures in this movement, particularly in the area of textile design and production, was William Morris. His firm, Morris & Co., produced a wide variety of printed and woven textiles and was instrumental in reviving traditional processes such as indigo discharge printing and vegetable dying. One of the first textile techniques he mastered was embroidery, which he learned in order to make bed-curtains and other hangings for his own home. The embroidery department of Morris & Co. offered designs for cushions, table covers, bed hangings, and other furnishing textiles, both as finished articles and in kit form.

From 1885 to 1896, Morris's daughter, May, a gifted designer in her own right, ran the embroidery department at Morris & Co. The portiere illustrated at left is one of a set of four curtains she designed about 1892–93. As in many of her other designs, the lush pattern of

fig. 20 In this photograph, taken while she was the head of Morris & Co.'s embroidery department, May Morris is dressed in the height of "artistic" fashion.

Portiere made from Morris & Co. *Oak* damask

May Morris (1862–1938)
England
1892–93
Silk damask, embroidered with silk, with silk fringe and cotton lining
259.1 x 137.2 cm (102 x 54 in.) including fringe
In memory of J. S. and Sayde Z. Gordon
from Myron K. and Natalie G. Stone   1983.160d

fruit trees and climbing vines gains added richness from the patterned ground fabric, a Morris & Co. silk damask designed by her father. The long, widely spaced stitches give the portiere a naive, handmade look, but they also show off the color and texture of the thick silk thread to best advantage and give the piece a shimmering, glowing quality. Silk is also the subject of the poem inscribed at the top, which continues onto the next curtain: "Lo silken my garden and silken my sky; And silken the apple boughs hanging on high...."

Another important firm in the development of Arts and Crafts textiles was the London retailer Liberty & Co. Arthur Lazenby Liberty founded the company in 1874, at first specializing in goods, particularly silks, imported from Asia. Within a few years, Liberty was working with English manufacturers to produce his own line of hand-printed "Liberty Art Silks," known for their distinctive "artistic" colors, such as peacock blue, sage, and willow green. In the early 1880s, Liberty's began to commission designs from leading professionals, including Charles Francis Annesley Voysey. C. F. A. Voysey had a successful career as an architect and furniture designer, but he was also known for his highly original fabrics and wallpapers. He designed the bedcover seen here about 1888; G. P. & J. Baker probably printed it for Liberty's several years later. The design, while clearly influenced by William Morris, displays Voysey's characteristic economy of line and his skill at composing patterns that are deliberately flat but never boring.

Bedcover
Designed by Charles Francis Annesley Voysey (1857–1941)
Printed by G. P. & J. Baker
Probably retailed by Liberty & Co.
England
Made about 1895; designed about 1888
Silk plain weave, block-printed
316 x 181.5 cm (124⁷/₁₆ x 71⁷/₁₆ in.)
Textile Income Purchase Fund   1976.764

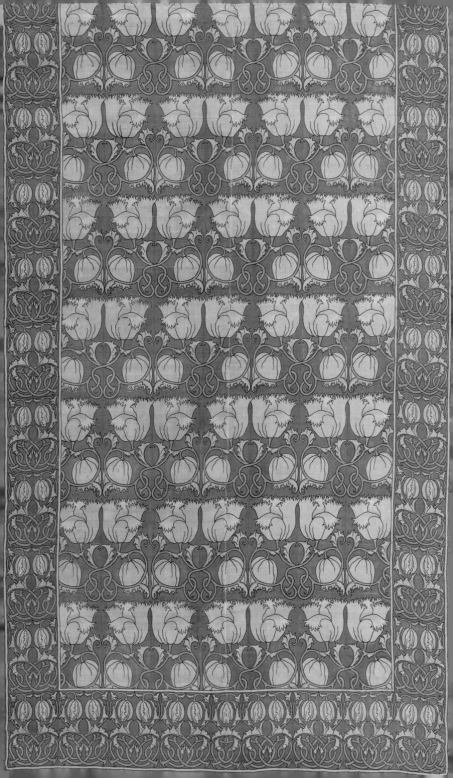

As part of its efforts to bring art into everyday life, the Arts and Crafts Movement also sought to reform fashion. The dress reformers of the late nineteenth century believed that modern women's fashions, with their restrictive corsets and heavy, voluminous skirts, were both unattractive and unhealthy. Seeking a more natural and aesthetic style of dress, many women in artistic circles, such as May Morris, began to wear loose, flowing gowns of ancient Greek, medieval, or early nineteenth-century inspiration, made of soft, gracefully draping fabric such as Liberty silk or velvet. In 1884 Liberty's opened its own costume department, which designed "Artistic" and "Picturesque" dresses and tea gowns, often featuring hand embroidery or smocking, and made them up in Liberty fabrics. This "Directoire"-style coat, embellished with embroidery in a medieval design, is a characteristic example of how Liberty's blended different historical and artistic influences to achieve a timeless style.

Woman's coat

Designed for Liberty & Co.

England (London)

About 1905

Silk satin with wool padding, embroidered
with silk floss and glass seed beads

Center back length: 149.9 cm (59 in.)

Textile Curator's Fund   2004.226

Ecclesiastical textiles were another area touched by the Arts and Crafts Movement, as Gothic Revival church architects sought to revive medieval craft traditions along with the Gothic style. Following the lead of A. W. N. Pugin, they began to design all of the furnishings for their churches, including woven fabrics, vestments, and hangings, and commissioned artisans to create them. Pugin and his followers modeled the embroidered elements of their vestments on those of the fifteenth and sixteenth centuries. As the skills needed to reproduce the fine gold work and figure embroidery of this period had been lost, new embroidery firms and volunteer societies for church embroidery were founded in order to revive them. Several Anglican religious societies, including the Society of the Sisters of Bethany, based in Lloyd Square, London, also established embroidery workrooms and schools. Sir J. Ninian Comper, an architect best known as a designer of church interiors and furnishings, designed many of the vestments the society embroidered, including the chasuble shown here. Although the chasuble was made about 1910, its clean, strong design and meticulous workmanship place it clearly within the nineteenth-century Arts and Crafts tradition.

SW

Saint Michael chasuble
Designed by Sir J. Ninian Comper (1864–1960)
Embroidered by the Society of the Sisters of Bethany
England (London)
About 1909–12
Silk damask with supplementary metal-wrapped patterning wefts, orphrey bands of silk damask embroidered with silk and metal-wrapped threads, and applied metallic braid
Center back length: 112.39 cm (44¼ in.)
The Elizabeth Day McCormick Collection, by exchange   1996.10

Art Deco Textiles

The term *Art Deco*, derived from the 1925 Exposition
Internationale des Arts Décoratifs et Industrials Mod-
ernes in Paris, was coined in the late 1960s to describe
a modern design style prevalent in architecture, decorative arts, fashion, and textiles of the 1910s to the
1930s. The style is broadly characterized by geometric
shapes, stylized motifs, and bold colors borrowed
from various "exotic" sources. These included the cultures of ancient Egypt, Central and South America,
China, and Japan, as well as avant-garde art movements such as Fauvism, Cubism, and Futurism. During the Art Deco period, numerous artists and
designers collaborated with one another and with
manufacturers, and the distinction between the fine
and decorative arts was blurred. France was the
undisputed leader in the luxury goods market and
produced many masterpieces in the field of fashion
and textiles. At the same time, a movement in the
United States sought to create an authentic, modern,
American aesthetic.

A quintessential motif of the early Art Deco style in
the 1910s and 1920s was the stylized rose, popularized
by the prolific French illustrator and designer Paul
Iribe. Iribe began his career as a typographer and car-
icaturist for various newspapers and magazines
before branching out into furniture, textile, jewelry,
wallpaper, and set design. Over the course of his
career, he worked in both France and the United States,
collaborating with numerous designers. The rose
appears, among other places, in textile designs he

fig. 21 **This fashion plate, one of
Paul Iribe's illustrations of the
French couturier Paul Poiret's first
solo fashion collection, includes
the iconic rose so closely associated with both designers.**

made for the luxury textile firm Bianchini-Férier, in Lyon. This 1914 fabric of pink and red roses in Neoclassical urns reflects Iribe's classically inspired aesthetic, as well as his unique and influential style of illustration, which mixed the line of Japanese woodcuts with colors used by the Fauve painters.

Large Parisian department stores were the arbiters of the new modern aesthetic in home furnishings of the 1920s. Through their art studios, which drew from the top echelon of French design talent, the stores disseminated modern design to the masses. They also sponsored ambitious pavilions at the 1925 Paris Exposition. French designer Maurice Dufrène created the dramatic textile at right for the department store Galeries Layfayette. Dufrène trained at the Ecole des Arts Décoratifs in Paris and was a founding member of the Salon des Artistes Décorateurs. He began as director of Galeries Layfayette's art studio, La Maîtrise, in 1921. This furnishing fabric, dating from about 1927, was designed to complement the streamlined furniture of the later Art Deco period. Its large-scale pattern of gray, pink, and off-white geometric forms displays Dufrène's preference for subtle color and evokes the dynamism of Futurist art. Subtle texture variations, produced by the complexity of the weave structure, give the piece a reflective surface and attest to the sophistication of French luxury textiles at this time.

A silk scarf (pp. 174–75) designed by American painter and textile artist Marguerite Zorach about 1918 shows the interest of the period's artists in borrowing from the arts of other cultures. Zorach created the scarf using a technique called batik, a traditional Indonesian wax-resist dye process that became popular in the West during the first decades of the twentieth century. Dutch trade and colonization in Java introduced the process to Europe, and the proliferation of "how-to" books on batik contributed to the technique's popularity with both amateur and professional artists.

Zorach studied painting in Paris and spent time in Asia (where she may have acquired tools for batik) before settling in New York City in 1912. Her travels abroad exposed her to the influences of Fauvist colors and Cubist geometry. However, frustrated by the limitations of painting, she turned to embroidery and batik to better capture the texture and intensity of color she sought to represent in her work. This scarf, as well as her embroideries and works on paper, displays her "primitive" and geometric figural compositions, reflecting her love of nature and everyday life. Zorach's works helped narrow the conventional gap between the fine and decorative arts.

TWH

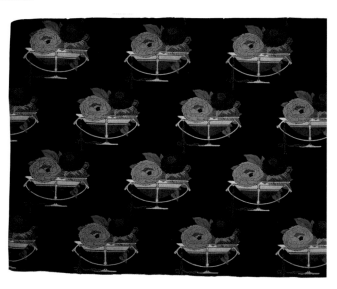

Length of furnishing or dress fabric
Paul Iribe (1883–1935) for Bianchini-Férier
France (Lyon)
About 1914
Silk satin, discharge-printed
59.1 x 87.6 cm (23 x 34 in.)
Alice M. Bartlett Fund   2001.817

Length of furnishing fabric

Maurice Dufrène (1876–1955)

France (Paris)

About 1927

Rayon and cotton jacquard

130.8 x 290.8 cm (51½ x 114½ in.)

Museum purchase with funds donated by

the Textile and Costume Society,

Museum of Fine Arts, Boston   2000.673

Scarf

Marguerite Zorach (1887–1968)

United States (New York City)

About 1918

Silk plain weave, wax-resist dyed (batik)

64.5 x 140 cm (25 3/8 x 55 1/8 in.)

Gift of Mrs. Alice B. Hornby 68.592

Postwar Couture

The Englishman Charles Frederick Worth had made Paris the capital of haute couture when he opened his fashion house there in 1857. During its first century, French couture dictated fashion trends and flourished as an industry. Its dominance culminated in the decade after World War II, often considered the golden age of French couture. Arguably the most influential trend to emerge from Paris fashion was Christian Dior's New Look, which debuted in his first line of 1947. The widespread popularity of Dior's line helped reestablish the preeminence of French couture, which had been diminished by the war when German-occupied Paris was isolated from the outside world and many French manufacturers and couture houses closed or decreased their output. The New Look consisted of soft, rounded shoulders, a cinched waist, padded hips, and full, long skirts. The silhouette was not new, but its opulence embodied a postwar optimism and notion of femininity that stood in stark contrast to the austere styles of the war years. The drama and artistry of couture garments, particularly eveningwear, created in the years following the end of the war reflect a revitalization of an industry committed to the highest quality craftsmanship.

Like Dior, Spanish-born Cristóbal Balenciaga was one of the most important couturiers of the postwar period. Known for his clean, modern, structured designs rooted in his training as a tailor, Balenciaga has been described as an architect of couture. His ensembles show his mastery of balance and proportion; their exquisite cut enhances a less-than-perfect

Evening dress
Cristóbal Balenciaga (Spanish, worked in France, 1895–1972) for the House of Eisa
Spain (Madrid)
1949
Silk plain weave (faille), appliquéd and embroidered with sequins, rhinestones, silk flowers and silk-wrapped wire, with silk net and silk plain weave lining
Center front length: bodice 35.6 cm (14 in.); center back length: skirt 118.1 cm (46 ½ in.)
Otis Norcross Fund   1999.281.1–3

figure, drawing attention to the curve of a neck or a delicate wrist. Always ahead of his time, Balenciaga had shown a version of the New Look silhouette in his late 1930s designs, and he introduced pillbox hats to his mid-1940s collections and the chemise or "sack" dress to his lines of the late 1950s; both became ubiquitous styles in the 1960s.

Balenciaga opened his first house in San Sebastian in 1916, followed by a number of other houses in Barcelona, Madrid, and Paris in the late 1920s and 1930s. In 1949 he created an evening dress (p. 177) for his Madrid house Eisa, named after his mother. It is a revival of a look from his much-acclaimed 1939 *Enfanta* collection, for which he interpreted garments from Spanish court portraits. The dress, which is made of ivory silk faille, displays Balenciaga's preference for fabrics with weight and body. Its color is in keeping with his striking use at that time of a limited color palette (early in his career he often worked with white, black, gray, and strong pinks). The embroidered, scallop-edged bodice, which was made by the firm Rebé and reflects Balenciaga's Spanish heritage, is three-dimensionally embellished with scroll-shaped passementerie, appliquéd pink silk flowers, sequins, and rhinestones.

Balenciaga once credited Charles James with raising dressmaking from an applied art form to a pure art form. Arguably the greatest American couturier, James rose to prominence in the 1940s and 1950s when most innovative American designers were making names for themselves in the ready-to-wear industry, which mass-manufactured their fashions for consumers to purchase in retail establishments. Although he made forays into ready-to-wear, James devoted his career to his limited body of custom designs. He is best remembered as a temperamental artist, poor businessman, and genius designer who employed mathematical precision to his garments. Self-taught, he first opened a millinery shop in Chicago in the early 1920s. He then worked in London and Paris in the 1930s, before relocating in 1939 to New York, where he remained until his death in 1978.

James's unembellished evening dresses are perhaps his greatest creations, showcasing his experimentation with draping, cutting, and construction techniques. For example, he placed seams in unexpected places that closely follow the curves of the body rather than employing more traditional two-dimensional, front and back construction. This gave his garments a three-dimensional quality, as illustrated in the sea-foam green dress shown here. The light green satin and taffeta dress is draped in such a way that the wearer's silhouette could look different, yet equally flattering, from every angle. Another dress of pearl gray chiffon over satin, also seen here, is more classically inspired in its design. Both gowns demonstrate James's ability to combine fabrics to great effect.

Evening dress (right)

Charles James (American, born in
England, 1906–1978)
United States (New York City)
1951
Silk plain weave (chiffon) and satin
Center back length: 142.9 cm (56 ¼ in.)
Museum purchase in honor of Elizabeth Ann Coleman,
David and Roberta Logie Curator of Textile and Fashion
Arts, 1998–2004, with funds donated by the Textile and
Costume Society, Museum of Fine Arts, Boston   2004.138

Evening dress (far right)

Charles James (American, born in
England, 1906–1978)
United States (New York City)
1950
Silk satin and plain weave (taffeta)
Center back length: 128.3 cm (50 ½ in.)
Museum purchase in honor of Elizabeth Ann Coleman,
David and Roberta Logie Curator of Textile and Fashion Arts,
1998–2004, with funds donated by the Textile and Fashion Arts
Visiting Committee, Museum of Fine Arts, Boston   2004.139

Madame Grès, née Germaine Emilie Krebs, also known as Alix Barton, was one of the most important female couturiers of the period. Born in Paris, Grès opened her first house under the name Alix Barton in 1934, closed it during the war, then reopened it as Madame Grès. She worked directly on the figure, carefully draping fabric to follow the lines of the body and employing intricate pleating techniques, as seen in this late 1950s evening dress. This asymmetric, knife-pleated, one-piece gown   is a classic example of her work. Panels of cream, pink, and light purple silk jersey form the braided bodice, then continue into the skirt; what appears to be the juncture of skirt and bodice is actually a stitching line holding the pleats in place. Elegant, classically inspired garments such as this reflect Grès's training as a sculptor and her individuality as a designer.

TWH

Evening dress
Madame Grès (1903–1993)
France (Paris)
Late 1950s
Silk knit (jersey)
Center back length: 124.5 cm (49 in.)
Arthur Tracy Cabot Fund   1998.434

Trapeze furnishing fabric

Printed by Laverne Originals

United States (New York City)

1950–54

Linen plain weave, screen-printed

274.3 x 116.8 cm (108 x 46 in.)

Textile Income Purchase Fund   2004.461

Midcentury Modern Textiles

In the decades after World War II, the clean lines, open plans, and glass walls of modern homes and office buildings brought about dramatic changes in furnishing fabrics and inspired a period of extraordinary creativity in textile design. Because many established textile firms were slow to adapt to changing requirements, the challenge of producing modern fabrics was taken up by a variety of small, idiosyncratic new manufacturers and design studios. Woven fabrics emphasized color and visible texture, and designers experimented with unusual materials, mixing handspun natural fibers with yarns made of nylon, lurex, or metal wire. Pattern designers found new sources of inspiration in modern art, architecture, and technology and created dynamic abstract designs based on photographic details of plants, whimsical chalk doodles, and scientific formulae. The press actively promoted modern fabric designs to the general public, and textiles were showcased in international design shows, at world's fairs, and in exhibitions such as the annual Good Design shows held at the Museum of Modern Art in New York. Although many of these avant-garde designs were expensive and not widely available, they strongly influenced the direction of postwar textile design and the appearance of modern interiors.

The American design firm Laverne Originals, founded in 1942 by the husband-and-wife team of painters Erwine and Estelle Laverne, specialized in hand-printed fabrics and wallpapers but also produced furniture and other decorative objects. The Lavernes continually sought out new ideas and approaches, both in their own designs and in those they commissioned from artists in other media, such as Alexander Calder and Ray Komai. Critics praised Laverne fabrics for their freshness and variety, and design journals and the popular press frequently featured them. *Trapeze*, one of their better-known designs, successfully combines two of the major themes of 1950s pattern design: strict geometry, represented by the green and yellow triangles, and freehand drawing (a characteristic Laverne touch), in the form of a mirror-image grid of hatched lines. The pattern's expansive scale made it an appropriate choice for the larger curtains required by modern floor-to-ceiling windows.

The Textilkammare (textile design studio) of the Stockholm department store Nordiska Kompaniet was another source of innovative designs. Its director from 1937 to 1971, designer Astrid Sampe, commissioned designs from a wide variety of fresh talents and well-known figures, including architects, ceramic and industrial designers, and even a Nobel Prize–winning chemist. One of the talented designers Sampe recruited was Viola Gråsten, who began her career as a designer of rya rugs in her native Finland. After moving to Sweden in the 1940s, Gråsten went to work for NK's Textilkammare, and in the 1950s she became one of its most important designers of printed textiles. Although primarily known for her sophisticated color sense and trademark glowing colors, Gråsten was equally successful working in minimalist black and white. The monumental *Ulmus* (Elm) is one of a famous series of large-scale designs inspired by trees, all in a minimal palette but remarkably varied in effect, which she developed for the Mölnlycke textile firm in the late 1950s.

Another pioneer in modern textile design was the Finnish company Marimekko, whose parent company, Printex Oy, was founded by Armi and Viljo Ratia in 1949. From its founding, Printex, under the artistic direction of Armi Ratia, printed abstract, nonfigurative, and unconventional designs and experimented with the possibilities of the screen-printing technique. Vuokko Eskolin-Nurmesniemi, the chief designer of fashion and fashion fabrics during the 1950s, brought daring combinations of brilliant color into the drabness of postwar Finland. She consciously used the areas where colors overlapped, traditionally considered a mistake in textile printing, to create composite colors—a device which became a Marimekko trademark. Many of the company's best-known and most influential designs, however, were the furnishing fabrics by Maija Isola, who designed for Printex and Marimekko from 1949 until 1987. Her bold, fluid, dramatically scaled designs of the 1960s, similar in spirit to contemporary "color field" paintings, revolutionized textile and interior design in the decades that followed. *Lokki* (Seagull), in which deceptively simple undulations of pure, flat color fill the whole width of the fabric, is among the earliest and most versatile of these designs (p. 186).

Jack Lenor Larsen has been one of the most influential furnishing-fabric designers of the postwar period. Larsen's textiles became known for their richness and variety and for the inventive and experimental processes employed in their manufacture, often combining machine and hand production. Beginning in the early 1950s, he and his studio found creative ways to adapt hand-woven designs to power looms, overcame the technical difficulties of printing on velvet, and specialized in durable, sheer drapery fabrics, such as a 1960 design of warp-knitted plastic film. The visual sophistication and technical innovation of Larsen's fabrics are epitomized by *Magnum* (p. 187), which Larsen and Win Anderson originally designed as a stage curtain for the Phoenix Civic Plaza–Concert Hall in Phoenix, Arizona. The pattern is a modernist interpretation of Indian mirror-work embroidery, densely machine embroidered in eight colors on a ground of heavy, padded mylar film. Extensive experimentation with materials and embroidery stitches was required to create this rich and colorful fabric, one of Larsen's most famous designs.

SW

***Ulmus* furnishing fabric**
Designed by Viola Gråsten (Swedish, born in Finland, 1910–1994)
for Mölnlycke Väfveri
Distributed by Nordiska Kompaniet's Textilkammare
Sweden
Designed 1957
Linen plain weave, screen-printed
274.3 x 132.1 cm (108 x 52 in.)
Textile Curator's Fund   2005.6

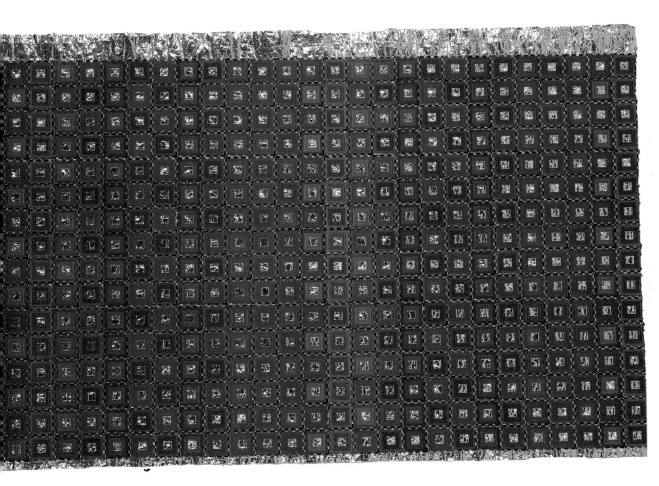

Lokki furnishing fabric

Designed by Maija Isola (1927–2001)

Manufactured by Marimekko

Finland

Designed 1961

Cotton plain weave, screen-printed

137.2 x 365.8 cm (54 x 144 in.)

Helen Moseley Fund   2002.674

© Marimekko Oyj

Magnum furnishing fabric

Designed by Jack Lenor Larsen (born in 1927)

and Win Anderson (born in 1922)

United States

1971–73

Silver mylar, machine embroidered with acrylic

135.3 x 246.4 cm (53¼ x 97 in.)

Museum purchase with funds donated by Doris May

and Suzanne W. and Alan J. Dworsky   2001.133

Geoffrey Beene

Geoffrey Beene created some of the most innovative, flattering, and comfortable clothing of the twentieth century. He was a master of cut and had an innate sense of pattern and texture. Throughout most of his career, he pushed the boundaries of how to cut clothing and experimented with new shapes and constructions, often putting him at odds with his employers and business partners. His search for independence eventually led to his break with the ready-to-wear industry, which was then, as it is now, located on Seventh Avenue between 30th and 42nd streets in New York. In 1989 he established a couture studio on West 57th Street, where he designed some of the most beautifully cut clothing of his career. The MFA is fortunate to have received from the artist a donation of over eighty ensembles, which he selected to represent his career.

Beene received his training in Paris just after World War II, attending the Chambre Syndicale de la Haute Couture and apprenticing with a tailor who worked for the couturier Edouard Molyneux. When he returned to New York, he worked for a series of ready-to-wear manufacturers, anonymously adapting Paris designs for the American market. By the early 1960s, American designers became celebrities in their own right and several, including Beene, opened houses under their own names. Geoffrey Beene Inc. opened in 1963 to great critical acclaim. Beene became known for well-cut, structured garments that hid a lot of figure flaws.

An evening dress from 1966 (p. 190, left) illustrates the simple cuts then in favor. Made of black wool knit, it also demonstrates Beene's interest in pushing the boundaries of what was accepted practice in the apparel industry. During the 1960s, knits, with their soft drape, were not commonly used for formal clothing. Originally popularized in the 1920s by Chanel, such fabric was associated with sportswear. Beene adapted it for eveningwear by studding it with rhinestones, a technique he also used on gray flannel and other daywear fabrics.

Societal and economic changes had reshaped the fashion world by the late 1960s. The increasing importance of the youth market and decreased consumer interest in following the dictates of name designers caused a real shake-up on Seventh Avenue. Those houses with strong designers who could adapt to the new marketplace, like Beene, managed to survive. Beene simplified his clothing by keeping similar shapes but removing the understructure. By the early 1980s, he became more conscious of the body beneath the garment, and his ideas of cut, comfort, and movement evolved from there.

A jumpsuit and bolero (p. 190, right) from his spring 1993 collection express many of Beene's design concepts of the time. The jumpsuit, although not the most practical female garment, is extremely comfortable and does not restrict the body. Beene's masterful combination of rayon jersey and linen provides contrast in texture and fit; the drape of the linen pants creates a volumetric foil for the fitted bodice and balances the single-seam bolero made of black and ivory silk satin. Beene used ballet dancers to model his spring 1993 collection, demonstrating his clothing's comfort and ease of movement.

The rest of his career was spent perfecting and refining his ideas. In 2001 Beene discontinued his ready-to-wear line and focused on custom-made clothing. His work routine resembled that of an artist more than a fashion designer, and the press referred to his ensembles as fine art. An evening dress from the 2001 spring collection (p. 191) is a study in triangles, a form Beene explored often in his career. He enjoyed playing with the shape and the way it worked with a woman's body. In this dress, he again contrasted linen and jersey. The black silk jersey flows over the body, while the linen shapes constructed into the bodice and skirt provide definition at the hips and waist. The dress is a masterwork of proportion and fit.

PAP

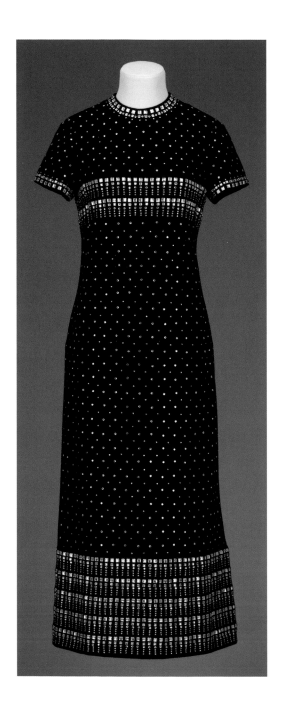

Evening dress (far left)

Geoffrey Beene (1927–2004)

United States (New York City)

1966

Wool knit with rhinestones

Center back length: 129.5 cm (51 in.)

Gift of Mr. Geoffrey Beene   2003.378

Jumpsuit and bolero (left)

Geoffrey Beene (1927–2004)

United States (New York City)

Spring 1993

Rayon knit (jersey), linen plain weave,

and silk double-faced satin

Center back length: jumpsuit

141 cm (55 ½ in.),

bolero 27.9 cm (11 in.)

Gift of Mr. Geoffrey Beene   2003.377.1–2

Evening dress (right)

Geoffrey Beene (1927–2004)

United States (New York City)

Spring 2001

Silk knit (jersey) and linen plain weave

Center back length: 109.2 cm (43 in.)

Gift of Mr. Geoffrey Beene   2004.694

Fiber Art

Fiber Art loosely refers to unique works of art emphasizing textiles or textile techniques. The term came into general use to describe the revolutionary experiments in sculptural woven forms of the 1960s, yet the emergence of fiber art can be traced to the years after World War II when artists began to create one-of-a-kind works of textile art. Two of the most influential pioneers in this field were Ed Rossbach and Katherine Westphal, husband and wife artists whose careers spanned five decades. Their innovative work, both as artists and teachers, and their lifelong advocacy of the creative process over the finished product opened the door to rich experimentation in textile art during the 1960s and 1970s.

During his long career, Rossbach created works in almost every known textile technique and format. Despite the variety in his work, certain themes prevailed, including an emphasis on structure, a delight in exploration, a questioning of expectations, an appreciation for historical textile techniques, and an enthusiasm for the expressive qualities of found materials. His exuberant approach to making art, free from expectations and rules, was tremendously influential on the generations of students he taught at the University of California, Berkeley.

Rossbach initially studied painting, design, and art education, not textiles. But during World War II, when he was stationed in the Aleutian Islands, he became fascinated by indigenous basket-making traditions, an interest he would maintain for the rest of his life. After the war he enrolled at the Cranbrook Academy of Art, where he acquired a formal, Bauhaus-based education in weaving. It was not until joining the staff of the Decorative Arts Department of the University of California, Berkeley, in 1950 that Rossbach launched into personal explorations of and innovation with textile techniques. He undertook in-depth analyses of the university's comprehensive collection of historical textiles, mastering the complex weaves in order to better instruct his students. He then reinterpreted these structures in his own art works.

His early pieces from the 1960s reflect his obsession with structural clarity. Often using labor-intensive techniques, such as discontinuous warp weaving, needle lace, or ikat dyeing, Rossbach created minimalist two-dimensional weavings that showcased these techniques. In one of his earliest pieces, *Reconstituted Commercial Textile*, from 1960, Rossbach manipulated the pattern in an ordinary commercial striped-print fabric by discharge printing and tie-dyeing it. He then encased the resulting fabric in plastic tubing and plaited it into a monochromatic, two-dimensional weaving.

Rossbach continued to experiment with structure in his later works but began to incorporate recognizable imagery and strong color, which aligned him more closely with the concurrent Pop Art movement. He also continued to plumb the expressive qualities of unconventional materials, such as newspaper, plastic garbage bags, and foil. *John Travolta* (p. 194), made in 1978, reveals Rossbach's more playful vein. It combines found materials such as electric tape, reeds, cotton twine, newspaper, and commercial silk organza with an image of a well-known pop icon.

What appears as a carelessly tied construction is really an expressive form unencumbered by the seriousness of high art.

Eschewing structure in favor of surface effects, Katherine Westphal has spent the better part of her career exploring complex visual layering. She received her B.A. and M.A. in painting from the University of California, Berkeley, and then spent eight years designing fabrics for the apparel industry. This early design experience for commercial industry led to formative explorations in her own artwork when she began to cut up and collage her leftover design samples. The results were complex two-dimensional works distinguished by fragmented images, layering, and collage techniques.

Westphal continued to pursue supplementary surface treatments, embellishing surfaces with an eclectic array of layered fabrics, overstitching, and even drawn and painted elements. She employed these techniques in a variety of forms, including quilts, jewelry, baskets, and two-dimensional embroideries. Westphal was an early proponent of color photocopy heat-transfer techniques. A photograph of her, taken in 1976 on the roof of the Basel Opera House in Switzerland, became the focal image of her 1978 art quilt *Hawaiian Kitsch* (p. 195). Freely manipulating the photograph through the process of color photocopy heat transfer, Westphal combined it with other photos of camels, pyramids, and hula dancers to create a lively and colorful collage on synthetic velvet.

LDW

Reconstituted Commercial Textile
Ed Rossbach (1914–2002)
United States
1960
Printed cotton plain weave, discharge-printed, tie-dyed, encased in polyethylene film tubing, and plaited
90.2 x 88.8 cm (35½ x 35 in.)
The Daphne Farago Collection
2004.2098

John Travolta
Ed Rossbach (1914–2002)
United States
1978
Heat-transfer-printed commercial silk
plain weave (organza), reeds, cotton
twine, electrical tape, and newspaper
40.6 x 22.9 x 17.8 cm (16 x 9 x 7 in.)
The Daphne Farago Collection   2004.428

Hawaiian Kitsch
Katherine Westphal (born 1919)
United States
1978
Synthetic velvet, photocopy heat-transfer-
printed, backed with cotton plain weave,
and quilted
228.6 x 142.2 cm (90 x 56 in.)
The Daphne Farago Collection   2004.2146

Glossary

appliqué: an embroidery technique in which shaped pieces of cloth are cut out and stitched onto the ground fabric.

batik: a technique of resist dyeing in which the pattern is formed by applying wax to areas of a fabric before dyeing. The wax is then removed by boiling the fabric in water, applying solvent to it, or ironing it on an absorbent surface.

brocade: see supplementary patterning wefts.

calico: a general term for a variety of printed cotton fabrics, first made in India and later in Europe and the United States.

chiffon: a very lightweight, sheer plain-weave silk fabric.

copperplate printing: the use of engraved copperplates to print a pattern on a textile.

couture: begun in France during the second half of the nineteenth century, a system of clothing production in which a designer creates several collections each year. Garments in the collection are sold to private clients and custom-made for each individual.

damask: a fabric in which the pattern is formed by the contrast between two different weave structures, such as a plain weave and a twill, or a satin and its reverse.

discharge printing: a method of printing with bleach or other color-destroying chemicals on dyed fabric in order to bleach out, or discharge, the color where the cloth is printed.

discontinuous warp and weft weaving: a general term for a weaving technique in which the warps and wefts do not run the full length or full width of the fabric.

faille: a plain-weave fabric with a ribbed surface, made by weaving fine, closely spaced warps with thicker wefts.

float: a portion of a warp or weft thread that passes over or under two or more of the opposite threads.

gimp: a decorative yarn made by wrapping silk, wool, cotton, or metal threads around a core of cord or wire. Used as trimming.

ikat: a technique in which the pattern is formed by resist dyeing the warp and/or weft of a fabric prior to weaving.

jacquard mechanism: a patterning mechanism attached to a loom and controlled by a series of punched cards.

jersey: a knit fabric in which the knitted loops are pulled to the back of the fabric. Also used generally to refer to any knitted fabric without a distinct rib.

lampas: woven fabric combining a ground weave (formed by a main warp and main weft) and a pattern weave (formed by a separate pattern warp and pattern weft).

mordant: a fixing agent, usually a metallic compound, used to fix a dye to a yarn or fabric. The use of a different mordant with the same dye can change or enhance how the dye is taken up by the yarn or fabric.

mulham: an Arabic term for a light fabric with a silk warp and a weft of a different fiber, often cotton.

passementerie: ornamental trimming, usually made of braid, cord, gimp, beads, etc., used on furnishings and clothing.

pile: yarns or fibers standing away from the surface of a fabric, usually created by cutting raised loops. In velvet, the pile loops are formed on the loom; in knotted pile structures, the pile yarns are individually tied onto the warps.

plain weave: the simplest weave structure, in which one weft thread passes over one warp thread and under the next, while the following weft thread passes under the first warp thread and over the next.

raffia (also spelled *raphia*): a fiber obtained from the leaf stalks of the raffia palm.

ready-to-wear: a general term for garments made in standardized sizes for retail sale (as opposed to custom-made garments).

repeat: the smallest design unit of a repeating pattern.

resist dyeing: a patterning technique in which sections of the warp and/or weft or finished cloth are covered prior to dyeing in order to prevent dye from penetrating. Varied substances and techniques can be used to resist the dye, including clamped wood blocks, ties, wax, and starch pastes.

samite (also spelled *samit*): a patterned textile with two or more supplementary wefts of different colors in addition to the main warp and weft woven in twill. The main warp controls which color supplementary weft appears on the front of the cloth and which on the back, creating the pattern.

satin: a weave structure with long warp floats (usually over four or more wefts

and under one) arranged to avoid the appearance of a diagonal pattern (see twill) and to form a smooth surface.

screen printing: method of fabric printing in which the pattern is produced by blocking out areas on a mesh screen. In hand screen printing, flat screens the width of one repeat are moved along the length of the fabric, and the color is forced through the screen with a squeegee. Each color requires a separate screen.

supplementary patterning wefts: the use of an extra weft, in addition to the main, structural weft, to create a pattern. Supplementary continuous patterning wefts travel from one selvedge, or finished edge, to the other. Supplementary discontinuous wefts are used only where they are needed for the pattern; they are not woven across the full width of the fabric. The term *brocade* is often used to refer to textiles patterned with supplementary discontinuous wefts.

taffeta: a ribbed plain-weave fabric (similar to faille, but lighter and more tightly woven), usually made of silk, with a smooth, crisp finish.

tapestry: a weave structure with one warp and wefts of different colors. Each weft color is used only where needed for the pattern. Different types of tapestry

are classed according to how the colored areas intersect: in interlocked tapestry, the wefts link around each other or around a common warp; in slit tapestry, the wefts pass around adjacent warps without linking, leaving a vertical slit; in dovetailed tapestry, wefts turn in groups of two or more around a common warp.

taqueté: a patterned textile with two or more supplementary wefts of different colors in addition to the main warp and weft woven in plain weave. The main warp controls which color supplementary weft appears on the front of the cloth and which on the back, creating the pattern.

tie-dyeing: a form of resist dyeing in which areas of fabric are gathered and tied tightly with string before dyeing. The tied areas resist the dye.

twill: a weave structure with warp and weft floats arranged in a diagonal order.

warp: the thread or threads that run lengthwise in a woven fabric. Warp threads are held parallel and under tension on the loom.

weft: the thread or threads that run across the width of the fabric, at right angles to the warp.

Further Reading

GENERAL

Jenkins, David, ed. *The Cambridge History of Western Textiles*. 2 vols. Cambridge: Cambridge University Press, 2003.

Steele, Valerie, ed. *Encyclopedia of Clothing and Fashion*. 3 vols. Detroit: Thomson Gale, 2005.

ANTIQUE AND MEDIEVAL TEXTILES

Paracas Textiles

Paul, Anne, ed. *Paracas Art and Architecture: Object and Context in South Coastal Peru*. Iowa City: University of Iowa Press, 1991.

Rowe, Ann Pollard. "Interlocking Warp and Weft in the Nasca 2 Style." *Textile Museum Journal* 3, no. 3: 67–78.

Late Antique Textiles

Arensberg, Susan MacMillan. "Dionysos: A Late Antique Tapestry." *Boston Museum Bulletin* 75 (1977): 4–25.

Tiwanaku-Style and Wari Textiles

Gallardo I., Francisco. *Identity and Prestige in the Andes: Caps, Turbans, and Diadems*. Santiago, Chile: Museo Chileno de Arte Precolombino, 1993.

Kolata, Alan L. *The Tiwanaku: Portrait of an Andean Civilization*. Cambridge, MA: Blackwell, 1993.

Medieval Islamic Textiles

Britton, Nancy Pence. *A Study of Some Early Islamic Textiles in the Museum of Fine Arts, Boston*. Boston: Museum of Fine Arts, 1938.

Partearroyo, Christina. "Almoravid and Almohad Textiles." In *Al-Andalus: The Art of Islamic Spain*, edited by Jerrilynn D. Dodds, 104–13. New York: Metropolitan Museum of Art, 1992.

Medieval Silks for the Church

Piponnier, Françoise, and Perrine Mane. *Dress in the Middle Ages*. Translated by Caroline Beamish. New Haven: Yale University Press, 1997.

Staniland, Kay. *Embroiderers*. Medieval Craftsmen Series. London: British Museum Press, 1991.

European Medieval Tapestries

Campbell, Thomas P., with contributions by Maryan W. Ainsworth et al. *Tapestry in the Renaissance: Art and Magnificence*. New York: Metropolitan Museum of Art; New Haven: Yale University Press, 2002.

Cavallo, Adolph S. *Tapestries of Europe and Colonial Peru in the Museum of Fine Arts, Boston*. Boston: Museum of Fine Arts, 1967.

THE AGE OF EXPLORATION

Postconquest Andean Textiles

Fane, Diane ed. *Converging Cultures: Art and Identity in Spanish America*. New York: Brooklyn Museum, 1996.

Phipps, Elena, Johanna Hecht, and Christina Esteras Martin. *The Colonial Andes: Tapestries and Silverwork, 1530–1830*. New York: Metropolitan Museum of Art; New Haven and London: Yale University Press, 2004.

Stone-Miller, Rebecca. *To Weave for the Sun: Andean Textiles in the Museum of Fine Arts, Boston*. Boston: Museum of Fine Arts, 1992.

Early Islamic Court Carpets

Denny, Walter. *Oriental Rugs*. New York: Cooper-Hewitt Museum, 1979.

King, Donald. *The Eastern Carpet in the Western World from the 15th to the 17th Century*. London: Arts Council of Great Britain, 1983.

Walker, Daniel. *Flowers Underfoot: Indian Carpets of the Mughal Era*. New York: Metropolitan Museum of Art, 1997.

Ottoman Textiles

Atasoy, Nurhan, Walter B. Denny, Louise W. Mackie, and Hülya Tezcan. *İPEK: The Crescent and the Rose, Imperial Ottoman Silks and Velvets.* London: Azimuth Editions, 2000.

Atıl, Esin. *The Age of Sultan Süleyman the Magnificent.* Washington, DC: National Gallery of Art; New York: Harry N. Abrams, 1987.

Baker, Patricia, Hülya Tezcan, and Jennifer Wearden. *Silks for the Sultans: Ottoman Imperial Garments from the Topkapi Palace.* Istanbul: Ertuġ & Kocabiyik, 1996.

Elizabethan Embroidery

Digby, George Wingfield. *Elizabethan Embroidery.* London: Faber and Faber, 1963.

King, Donald, and Santina Levey. *Embroidery in Britain from 1200 to 1750.* London: Victoria and Albert Museum, 1993.

Synge, Lanto. *Art of Embroidery: History of Style and Technique.* Woodbridge, Suffolk: Antique Collector's Club, 2001.

Flowers of Mughal India

Ames, Frank. *The Kashmir Shawl and Its Indo-French Influence.* 3rd ed. Woodbridge, Suffolk: Antique Collector's Club, 1997.

Desai, Vishakha N. *Life at Court: Art for India's Rulers, 16th–19th Centuries.* Boston: Museum of Fine Arts, Boston, 1985.

Victoria and Albert Museum. *The Indian Heritage: Court Life and Arts under Mughal Rule.* London: Victoria and Albert Museum, 1982.

Chinese Dragon Robes

Vollmer, John E. *Ruling from the Dragon Throne: Costume of the Qing Dynasty (1644–1911).* Berkeley: Ten Speed Press, 2002.

Early Eighteenth-Century European Silks

Maeder, Edward, et al. *An Elegant Art: Fashion and Fantasy in the Eighteenth Century.* Los Angeles and New York: Los Angeles County Museum of Art and Harry N. Abrams, 1983.

Ribeiro, Aileen. *Dress in Eighteenth-Century Europe, 1715–1789.* New York: Holmes & Meier, 1984.

Colonial Boston Embroidery

Ring, Betty. *Girlhood Embroidery: American Samplers and Pictorial Needlework, 1650–1850.* 2 vols. New York: Alfred A. Knopf, 1993.

Rowe, Ann Pollard. "Crewel Embroidered Bed Hangings in Old and New England." *Boston Museum Bulletin* 71 (1973): 102–63.

TRADITION AND INDUSTRY

The Fashionable Fan

Bennett, Anna Gray. *Unfolding Beauty: The Art of the Fan.* Boston: Museum of Fine Arts, Boston, 1988.

Costumes for the Nō Theater

Nagasaki, Iwao, Monica Bethe, et al. *Patterns and Poetry: Nō Robes from the Lucy Truman Aldrich Collection at the Museum of Art, Rhode Island School of Design.* Providence: Rhode Island School of Design, 1992.

Takeda, Sharon Sadako, and Monica Bethe. *Miracles and Mischief: Noh and Kyōgen Theater in Japan.* Los Angeles: Los Angeles County Museum of Art, 2002.

American Quilts

Bassette, Lynn, and Jack Larkin. *Northern Comfort: New England's Early Quilts.* Nashville: Rutledge Hill Press, 1998.

Brackman, Barbara. *Clues in the Calico: A Guide to Identifying and Dating Antique Quilts.* McLean, VA: EPM Publications, 1989.

Peck, Amelia. *American Quilts and Coverlets in the Metropolitan Museum of Art*. New York: Metropolitan Museum of Art and Dutton Studio Books, 1990.

European Printed Textiles

Brédif, Josette. *Toiles de Jouy*. New York: Rizzoli, 1989.

Montgomery, Florence. *Printed Textiles: English and American Cottons and Linens, 1750–1850*. New York: Viking Press, 1970.

Robinson, Stuart. *A History of Printed Textiles*. Cambridge, MA: MIT Press, 1969.

Siegele, Starr. *Toiles for All Seasons: French & English Printed Textiles*. Boston: Bunker Hill Publishing in association with Allentown Art Museum, 2004.

Early to Mid-Nineteenth-Century Fashion

Byrde, Penelope. *Nineteenth-Century Fashion*. London: B. T. Batsford, 1992.

Cunnington, Phillis Emily. *Costumes of the Nineteenth Century*. Boston: Plays, 1970.

Foster, Vanda. *A Visual History of Costume: The Nineteenth Century*. London: B. T. Batsford, 1984.

Textiles from Sub-Saharan Africa

Coquet, Michèle. *Textiles Africains*. Paris: Adam Biro, 1998.

Picton, John. *African Textiles: Looms, Weaving and Design*. London: British Museum Publications, 1979.

Ross, Doran H. *Wrapped in Pride: Ghanaian Kente and African American Identity*. Los Angeles: UCLA Fowler Museum of Cultural History, 1998.

Greek Islands Embroideries

Krody, Sumru Belger. *Embroidery of the Greek Islands and Epirus Region: Harpies, Mermaids, and Tulips*. Washington, DC: Textile Museum, 2006.

MacMillan, Susan. *Greek Islands Embroideries*. Boston: Museum of Fine Arts, 1974.

Taylor, Roderick. *Embroidery of the Greek Islands*. New York: Interlink Books, 1998.

Trilling, James. *Aegean Crossroads: Greek Island Embroideries in the Textile Museum*. Washington, DC: Textile Museum, 1983.

Sumatran Textiles

Gittinger, Mattiebelle. *Splendid Symbols: Textiles and Tradition in Indonesia*. New ed. Singapore and New York: Oxford University Press, 1985.

Summerfield, Anne, and John Summerfield, eds. *Walk in Splendor: Ceremonial Dress and the Minangkabau*. Los Angeles: UCLA Fowler Museum of Cultural History, 1999.

THE MODERN WORLD

Worth and the Birth of Couture

Coleman, Elizabeth Ann. *The Opulent Era: Fashions of Worth, Doucet, and Pingat*. Brooklyn: The Brooklyn Museum in association with Thames and Hudson, 1989.

Milbank, Caroline Rennolds. *Couture: The Great Designers*. New York: Stewart, Tabori & Chang, 1985.

The English Arts and Crafts Movement

Johnstone, Pauline. *High Fashion in the Church*. Leeds: Maney Publishing, 2002.

Morris, Barbara. *Liberty Design, 1874–1914*. London: Pyramid Books, 1989.

Parry, Linda. *Textiles of the Arts and Crafts Movement*. New ed. London: Thames and Hudson, 2005.

Art Deco Textiles

Benton, Tim. *Art Deco: 1910–1939*. London: V&A Publications, 2003.

Hardy, Alain-René. *Art Deco Textiles: The French Designers*. London and New York: Thames and Hudson, 2003.

Samuels, Charlotte. *Art Deco Textiles*. London: V&A Publications, 2003.

Postwar Couture

Coleman, Elizabeth Ann. *The Genius of Charles James*. Brooklyn: Brooklyn Museum, 1982.

Healy, Robyn. *Balenciaga: Masterpieces of Fashion Design*. Melbourne, Victoria: National Gallery of Victoria, 1992.

Jouve, Marie-Andrée. *Balenciaga*. New York: Rizzoli, 1989.

Martin, Richard. *Madame Grès*. New York: Metropolitan Museum of Art, 1994.

Palmer, Alexandra. *Couture and Commerce: The Transatlantic Fashion Trade in the 1950s*. Vancouver: UBC Press, 2001.

Midcentury Modern Textiles

Aav, Marianne, ed. *Marimekko: Fabrics, Fashion, Architecture*. New Haven: Yale University Press, 2003.

Hiesinger, Kathryn B., and George H. Marcus, eds. *Design since 1945*. Philadelphia: Philadelphia Museum of Art, 1983.

Jackson, Lesley. *Twentieth-Century Pattern Design*. New York: Princeton Architectural Press, 2002.

Geoffrey Beene

Luther, Marylou, Pamela A. Parmal, and James Wolcott. *Beene by Beene*. New York: Vendome, 2005.

Fiber Art

Constantine, Mildred, and Jack Lenor Larsen. *Beyond Craft: The Art Fabric*. New York: Van Nostrand Reinhold, 1973.

Rossbach, Ed. *Ed Rossbach: 40 Years of Exploration and Innovation in Fiber Art*. Asheville, NC: Lark Books; Washington, DC: Textile Museum, 1990.

Smith, Paul J. *Ties That Bind: Fiber Art by Ed Rossbach and Katherine Westphal from the Daphne Farago Collection*. Providence: Museum of Art, Rhode Island School of Design, 1997.

Figure Illustrations

1 Length of velvet (detail)
Italy
15th century
Silk velvet, brocaded with gold metallic thread
110 x 239 cm (43¼ x 94 in.)
Gift of Philip Lehman "in memory of
my wife Carrie L. Lehman" 38.1041

2 *Penelope at Her Loom* (detail)
France or Flanders
About 1480–83
Wool slit tapestry
155 x 95 cm (61 x 39¾ in.)
Marie Antoinette Evans Fund 26.54

3 Weaver's workbasket and implements
Peru (Central Coast, Chancay)
Late Intermediate period, 1000–1476
Plaited reed basket with wood spindles, whorls,
picks, shed sticks, bobbins, skein of cotton, camelid fiber,
ceramic dish, bone pick, spine needle, and chalk
Basket: 32.5 x 13.7 x 9.5 cm (12¾ x 5½ x 3¾ in.)
Gift of Charles H. White 02.680

4 Textile commemorating the Great Exhibition
of 1851 (detail)
England
About 1851
Printed cotton plain weave
64 x 37 cm (25¼ x 14½ in.)
Gift of Mrs. H. K. Estabrook 41.659

5 Photograph of the Museum's Textile Study Room
About 1911
Museum of Fine Arts, Boston

6 Detail of colonial-period cover, 11.1264 (see pp. 66–67)

7 Detail of *Wild Men and Moors*, 54.1431 (see pp. 54–55)

8 Photograph of Gertrude Townsend leading a tour of the
Elizabeth Day McCormick collection
1944
Museum of Fine Arts, Boston

9 Photograph of the exhibition "She Walks in Splendor"
1963
Museum of Fine Arts, Boston

10 Photograph of the exhibition "She Walks in Splendor"
1963
Museum of Fine Arts, Boston

11 Oil flask (lekythos) with a woman working wool (detail)
Brygos painter
Greece (Athens)
Early Classical period, about 480–470 B.C.
Red-figure ceramic
Height: 32.2 cm (13 in.)
Francis Bartlett Donation of 1912 13.189

12 Folding fan (detail)
China
Late 18th century
Ivory and paper with watercolor
Length of guard: 26 cm (10¼ in.)
Oldham Collection 1976.393

13 Platform shoes
Vivienne Westwood (born in 1941)
England
1991
Printed cotton twill, wood, and leather
20.3 x 7.6 x 21.6 cm (8 x 3 x 8½ in.)
Textile Income Purchase Fund 2002.672.1–2

14 Reverse of embroidered picture, 59.22 (see p. 100)

15 Embroidered petticoat border (detail)
New England colonies (probably Boston)
1725–50
Linen and cotton plain weave, embroidered with wool
192.7 x 21 cm (78 x 8¼ in.)
John Wheelock Elliot Fund   25.186a

16 Illustration of ladies sewing (detail)
Adachi Ginkō (worked 1874–1897)
Japan
Meiji era, 1887
Woodblock print; ink, color, and silver on paper
Vertical *ōban* triptych; each sheet: 36.5 x 25.2 cm (14⅜ x
9¹⁵⁄₁₆ in.)
William Sturgis Bigelow Collection   11.18171

17 Length of fabric (detail)
India (Coromandel Coast)
1725–75
Cotton plain weave, block-printed
110 x 65.5 cm (43¼ x 25¾ in.)
Helen and Alice Colburn Fund   27.800

18 "Le Ruban Employé dans la Mode et la Couture"
(The Ribbon as Employed in Fashion and the Couture),
from *Gazette du Bon Ton*
France (Paris)
April 1922
Engraving with hand-applied color (*pochoir*)
25.4 x 19 cm (10 x 7½ in.)
Transferred from the William Morris Hunt Memorial
Library   2004.48.11

19 Label from a dress (detail)
Worth and Bobergh
France (Paris)
About 1870
Stamped silk twill
Gift of Lois Adams Goldstone   2002.696.1–5

20 Photograph of May Morris
Frederick Hollyer (1837–1933)
About 1887–90
William Morris Gallery, London

21 Plate from *Les Robes de Paul Poiret racontées par Paul Iribe*
(Paul Poiret's Gowns Described by Paul Iribe)
Paul Iribe (1883–1935)
France (Paris)
1908
Relief etching on laid paper with hand-applied color
32.7 x 30.2 cm (12⅞ x 11⅞ in.)
Museum purchase with funds donated by Mrs. Roberta
Logie   1998.2

Index

*Page numbers in italics
indicate illustration captions.*

Powers, Harriet, 124, *127*
Printed textiles, European, 130–33
Printex Oy, 184, *186*
Pugin, A. W. N., 169

Quianlong emperor, 92–93
Quilts, 122–29

Raffia (raphia), 139–40, *141*
Rathbone, Perry, 20
Ratia, Armi and Viljo, 184
Reconstituted Commercial Textile (Rossbach), 192, *193*
Relic bag fragment, 50, *50*, 51
Repeats, design, 95, 131, 132
Reticella lace, 111
Robes, Chinese, 90–93, *90*, *92*, *93*
Robe volante dress style, 97, *97*
Rosenstein, Nettie, 19, 20
Ross, Denman Waldo, 8, 15
Rossbach, Ed, 157, 192–93, *193*, *194*
Roundels, 41, *42*
Ruskin, John, 157
Rustam (warrior hero), 76

Sacque dress, 97, *97*
Safavid dynasty, 68, 70
Saint Bonaventure, 48
Saint Michael chasuble, 169, *169*
Saint Peter, Benedictine monastery of, 44, 46
Sampe, Astrid, 183
Sampler, 104, *105*
San Pedro de Osma, 40, 43, *43*
Sarong, or skirt (*tapis*), 106–7, 150, *152*
Sashes (*patka*), 85, *88*, 89, *89*
Scarf, 172, *174–75*
Second Council of Lyons, 48
Seraser fabric, 74, 76, 77
Sewing machines, 109, *109*
Shawls, 85, *87*
"She Walks in Splendor: Great Costumes, 1550–1950," *19*, 20
"Ship cloths," 150, *150–51*
Shoes, *95*
Shrouds, *40*, 43, *43*, *62*, 63–64, *63*
Silk fragment with shepherd, 33, *35*
Silks, early eighteenth-century European, 94–97

Simpson, Adele, 19
Sisters of Bethany, Society of, 169
Skirts, women's ceremonial, *106–7*, 150, *152*, 140, *142–43*
Slit tapestries, *17*, *22–23*, 52, *52–53*, *54–55*, *90–91*
Sloman, Heinrich, 95
Smith, Jennie, 124
South Kensington School and Museum, 14–15
Sovey, Raymond, 20
Spain, 43, 177–78
Stomacher, 96, *96*
Sub-Saharan African textiles, 138–43
Sumatran textiles, 150–53
Sweden, 183–84

Tapestries, *10*, *17*, *22–23*, *36*, *37*, 52–57, *90–91*
Tapis (ceremonial skirt), *106–7*, 150, *152*
Taqueté weave structure, 76, *76–77*
Tassanari & Chatel, 160
Tawney, Lenore, 157
Textile collections, history of, 13–17
Textile Study Room, MFA, 15, *15*, 17
Textilkammare, Nordiska Kompaniet, 183–84
Tibet, 91–93
Tie-dyeing, 192
Tiwanaku-style textiles, *36*, 37
Tocapu motifs, *62*, *63*, 64
Tools, Peruvian textile-making, *12*
Townsend, Gertrude, 17, *18*, 19, 21
Trapeze furnishing fabric (Laverne Originals), *182*, 183
Travolta. *See John Travolta* (Rossbach)
Tribe, Paul, *154–55*, 171–72, *171*, *172*
Turkey, 76, 145
Two textile lengths, stitched together, *94*, 95–96

Ulmus furnishing fabric (Gråsten), 184, *185*
United States of America, *12*, 98–105, 123–29, 134, 171, 172, 178, 183, 184, 189
University of California, Berkeley, 192, 193

van Leeuwenhock, Anton, 95
Velvet, lengths of, *11*, 74, *75*
Victoria and Albert Museum, 14–15, 20
Voysey, Charles Francis Annesley, 166, *167*
Vreeland, Diana, 19